Whose Time Is It, Anyway?

Whose Time Is It, Anyway?

One Man's View of Our Human Experience

Chet Morelli

iUniverse, Inc.

New York Lincoln Shanghai

Whose Time Is It, Anyway?
One Man's View of Our Human Experience

iUniverse books may be ordered through booksellers or by contacting:

iUniverse
2021 Pine Lake Road, Suite 100
Lincoln, NE 68512
www.iuniverse.com
1-800-Authors (1-800-288-4677)

ISBN: 978-0-595-43367-4 (pbk)
ISBN: 978-0-595-87692-1 (ebk)

Printed in the United States of America

Contents

Introduction

In this book we shall journey through Time: The Past, Present, and a possible Future. We will look at the believable and the unbelievable, some facts and some fiction, the remarkable, and things that seem to be so absurd as to be unreal … or, could they be true? We will look at information that is verifiable, and information that is speculative.

On this ride in time, we will travel through historical records, scientific insight, medical information, archeological evidence, myths, legends, Angels, demons, UFO's, and the Heavens! We will also visit the Great Pyramid in Egypt, with a quick stop at the Lost Civilization of Atlantis, and a walk into the Future on "The Planet of the Plug-Ins, 2111 AD!"

Mankind has done so many great things; then again on the other side of our history, it is littered with war … Why? We shall look at the possible answers!

On the clock of human experience, we shall explore our thoughts about life, death, the afterlife, and God. What have we done in the Past, what are we doing in the Present, and what could we end up doing in the Future?

Whose Time Is It Anyway is a book that will probably raise more questions than it will answer, or it may answer some of the enigmas in time! This book may also get you to think about our human experience as time has, is, and will go on. In the following pages are my thoughts, views, and honest speculations about our past, the present, and the future.

What is time? According to the insights of Dr. Albert Einstein, time is a physical property that changes with mass, speed, and gravity. This means that the faster an object travels in outer-space time will slow down for the object. This does not happen on Earth because gravity keeps time at a constant. We here on the Earth measure the movement of time with clocks, the eternal watch forever ticking forward, … or is it? Time is not something we can really see or touch, we can only use it. I believe that time has a mind of its own, and we are all in it together!

Think about this: If you sit and watch the clock for one hour, time will move slowly, if you do not watch the clock, the hour will move quickly. Same one hour, moving at two different speeds. Is this the mind of time at work on the mind of man?

The good Dr. Einstein once said this about time, "The distinction between the past, present, and the future are all but a stubborn illusion." What this statement is saying, is that: "all three clocks are running simultaneously!" A cosmic harmony, of what was, what is; and what will be. The eternal balance of time that we are all a part of, this of course leads to the following questions:

Where have we come from? Where are we now? Where are we going?

That all depends on Whose Time Is It Anyway? Enjoy the Journey ...

THE CLOCKS OF TIME START NOW!

Chapter One

Clock One: Our Past Human History ... How much do we really know?

Origins: What Did the Ancients Believe?

The summer sun rises on the dawn of civilization. An intelligent human race emerges abruptly on Earth, as had not been seen before. These are the Ancients! On this nice summer morning in the cradle of life, somewhere in the Middle East so many eons ago, what did they think, and believe about their origins? Have they left us any clues to their thoughts and beliefs?

In the evidence from ancient writings let's see what we <u>do not</u> find in their understandings about mans origins. Has man evolved over millions of years? Well the earliest Ancients never ask that question according to their writings, the first thoughts on evolution are Greek, about 300 B.C. or so, then Darwin did a lot of speculating about the "origin of species," and he reintroduced this theory in around the 1860's AD. As for the majority of the Ancients, they did not believe in evolution, as most all of their writings show a belief in God, or the gods. Were they uninformed about the ascent of man as modern science teaches?

Outer Space is a modern term the Ancients were well aware of, but they called this place: "the Heavens." From Stonehenge, on the Salisbury Plain, to the Great Pyramid in Egypt, across the ocean to the Mayan Temples, our planet has astronomical observatories from antiquity that are all over the place! These guys were professional stargazers, always watching the skies. Why and what were they looking for? Did they believe that we came from the stars and are destined to return to our origins in space? Part of what we know is this; they were calculating with great accuracy all the movements in the sky from many different locations on the earth.

The sun has hit Stonehenge at the summer solstice in the same spot for over 4000 years, or longer! The Great Pyramid standing in time, with mathematical precision, and an eye to the sky, saying to all generations, "Come, Look, and Study Me, I'm Special!" Are these great monuments evidence that the Ancients were watching the sky and waiting for space-aliens? These master stargazers of the past were peering through the window of heaven, always calculating movements and measuring time. Was this because they were waiting for beings from other galaxies to show up?

The answer, from recorded history ... is No. They were looking for beings all right, not in outer space, they were looking in the Heavens; and they were looking for GOD, or the gods! From the sun god of Egypt, and dragon gods of China, there are Zeus, Apollo, Jupiter and Mars from the Greeks and Romans, all of these are gods in antiquity.

Wait, there's more, the Babylonians had 360 gods, one for each day of their year. A lot of celebrating going on in Babylon, how would you like to own the Babylon Card Co.? Ka-Ching ... Ah, capitalism, or was it a "here a god, there a god" money trick at its finest, in 3000 BC.!

[There are those today that lead others to many different gods, all for money and control. Don't believe me, just look at all the new-age Hollywood "fad gods" that come and go, along with people's cash! Look below at how the Ancients viewed the gods and see if they parallel some of the "fads" in our society today.]

In mans history the gods were everywhere and in almost anything. According to these people the gods were in control of everything and everyone, they made the heavens, the earth and they sustained them. The gods were worshiped and feared, loved and hated, all because they could bring good things upon earth, for mankind to enjoy, ... or these gods could bring about chaos and destroy the planet. These are some of the reasons why the Ancients left us with so much written information that the gods were to be feared and revered for who they were and what they did, the creators and givers of life, the destroyers and bringers of death. The benevolent or malevolent gods of old are still called on by the Ancients through the corridors of time to us today, and many people answer these gods by believing in them; even in our modern age!

If we take a close look at our professional sky watchers in days of old, they were looking beyond what we today call outer space. They were looking into the heavens. They were looking for their gods. Were these people all stupid and superstitious, or was there some truth to all of this? They seemed to believe that there is more to our reality than meets the eye. [Many of us today feel that there is more to our reality also, and our faith in one GOD proves this!]

Is there historical evidence for ancient beliefs in a one Divine GOD? A divine God who created the universe, and man, for a mightier purpose; with more to life than our earthly walk in time! Of course there is evidence for this, and our three main beliefs of today about origins come from antiquity. The Jewish TORAH, the Christian BIBLE, and Islam's Qu'ran all have a "Creator GOD" as the focal point of each of these belief systems: He {GOD} has made man here on earth for a "divine" purpose, with an ultimate plan. The ancient records indicate that they were for the most part creationists, as many people are to this day.

These are some of the beliefs of the Ancients about our origins. Our ancient ancestors believed that we came from the GOD or we were made by the gods. Could these men and women of old all be bona fide nut cases for not understanding evolution and space aliens?

THINK ABOUT THIS:

In the year 2007 the jury is still debating the origins of man. Is it just a cosmic accident, or is this all a master plan? Did GOD create us, or have we ascended from the apes; then again, did the space aliens do it, and our ancestors thought them to be the gods; ... or maybe we are just a cosmic "blip" on the radar screen of the universe?

"For a man who believes in nothing, then nowhere is just as good as any place to be. For a man who believes in something, he will have a certain place to be!"

In the hour glass of time more grains of sand seem to be creationists. What kind of grain of sand are you?

Shall I continue in the defense of GOD, or the gods? I think not for they are mightier than we; they can speak for themselves in each person's mind and heart. The mind says, "Show me; then I will believe," while the heart says, "I believe, therefore I see."

How Long Have We Been Here On Earth?

Where did the concept and knowledge come from to begin "ticking away the time?" We know many ancient cultures had ways for measuring time. Who started keeping time on earth? Well some historical evidence points to the Babylonians from about 4000 years ago, and we might still be using some of their methods today. Such as, sixty seconds in a minute, twenty-four hours in a day, these measurements are most likely from Babylon. This city goes all the way back through Biblical times and the Bible has about the same date for this city, which is about 2000 BC. Here science and the Bible agree that there is a city named Babylon that is about 4000 years old.

Does this mean we have only been on earth for 4000 years, or so? No, that is not what modern science teaches today, but to the Ancients and the Bible this was close to the beginning of time.

All over the globe there is archeological evidence for the sudden appearance of a very intelligent human race arriving on earth between 6000 and 10,000 BC. How old did the Ancients think they were? Remember these guys were darn good at math.

Most of the earliest cultures thought that time started with them, and set the beginning of time, at year # One. To some of them about 6,000 years ago was close to year # One, this would make the date about 4000 B.C. Looking through some modern archeological evidence, ancient writings, and a few very old belief systems, some researchers use this time as the approximate date for the arrival of "intelligent" human beings here on the earth.

So, are we now saying that man has only been here for 6,000 years? No, how could we say that when the geological records are assumed to show a planet that is billions of years old, with man evolving in the cosmos, even though neither one has been proven scientifically to be totally true,.. if at all!

Our ancestors who had the insight to start the clock in the first place, had a feeling they were close to the beginning of creation. As time has moved forward to 2007, we can see they were right. They are at the start of recorded human history!

In the Ancient cultures time itself was believed to start with the rise of these earliest time keepers. Strange thing is, most start keeping time between 1000 and 3000 BC. Oh; this gets better, because there are at least two Holy Books that have dates in them on when time began. These books are: the Torah, and the Bible, and they have dates for the beginning of time at about 4000 BC. Again, this fits together with some of the archeological dating that shows evidence that "intelligent men and women" were here on earth about 5000 to 10,000 years ago. These dates from the Bible, the Torah, and archeology overlap at around 6000 years ago [4000 BC], ... here look at this:

Two different modern cultures are to this day using calendars that go back to their beginnings, the Chinese calendar is counting the years, and yes, their calendar started about 6000 years ago, on the Hebrew calendar it is close to the year 5800! Is all of this a coincidence that these dates are all in the same vicinity?

Could it be that the human race as we are today is only 6000 years old? That would mean the clock started ticking in 4000 BC. Does this prove that we are possibly only thousands of years old? No, this does not prove how long we have been here. This is what the Bible, and some of the Ancients believed; and also at about this same time man started to record his own human history. All just a coincidence, I personally do not think so!

The question is what do you believe today on how long man has been here? Is it millions of years or just thousands of years? Modern man with science says millions, but the Ancients, and two ancient Holy Books, say thousands. Both can not be correct. Are the scientist's, archeologists, and the researchers not looking at the evidence correctly?

THINK ABOUT THIS:

Master mathematician's who were there to start-up the clock of time; the first tics were from their hands. They longed to be forever young, and they were young when all this human activity started on planet earth. When time began to be recorded with these people that we call very old, who started counting so very long ago, in a time that the Bible calls the beginning. How did these Ancient math wizards count? Well, when we count we always start with the number one. They probably counted the same way. Let's count: and a year one (4000 BC), and a two, and a three, and a 2007, WOOPS: 6000 years of time sure flies, doesn't it, when you count from the beginning!

What Did Our Human Ancestors See While They Were Here On Earth?

Why is ancient history filled with all kinds of strange, bizarre, abnormal creatures, and beings? What about all the weird events associated with them? Did the Ancients really see things like, angels, demons, fire breathing-flying dragons, and creatures, that were half man and half animal, [were there Demo-creeps and Repel-a-cans in the past also? oh no, these creatures would come later!]

Have UFO's been with us since the Dawn of Civilization, and our ancestors thought that they were the gods, or from God? Are they foretold to return someday from outer-space? Are these entities really coming from the pages of the Bible, and are they the angels and demons of scripture? Why is so much of the ancient record devoted to this twilight-zone stuff?

The big problem is that these beings, creatures, and events are in all civilizations and cultures, all throughout time; and all over the planet! Even people in our day report UFO encounters, and all kinds of weird paranormal activities! Is everyone who has had these experiences throughout time in the "twilight zone?" I personally don't think so; there are too many reports of these "strange" events and encounters in our time, and in ancient times. In my opinion there must be some truth to this "strange stuff."[Remember that the "truth" is always "stranger" than "fiction"]

Has GOD Himself come down to the earth early in mans recorded history? Some Holy Books from antiquity say exactly that; yes GOD has come down from heaven to visit man here on the earth. There are also oral traditions with American Indians, who to this day pray to the Great Spirit, their great God, who is said to come and visit His people. The Hebrew TORAH has the Divine GOD who proclaimed "Let Light Be," and then "walked" in the Garden of Eden with Adam and Eve. Two Gods of old and both are said to have come down to earth. [Maybe one of them is going to return soon!]

Moses is said to have seen GOD, face to face in the tabernacle by Mt. Horeb, in the Holy Land! In the Bibles book of Exodus, (King James Version) chapter 33, verse11, we read this "And the Lord spoke to Moses face to face;"

[Mind food for thought: Who was Moses talking to, was he seeing things, and hearing voices? Strange thing is we have the Ten Commandments, which were written down by Moses as given to him from God. Words of truth that worked in Moses' day, if only we would use them in our day, ... we all know the world would be a better place if we would listen to GOD through Moses. [To this day The Ten Commandments are posted above our Supreme Court of the United States, and this Court seems to ignore these time tested truths! Just look at some of their "Godless" rulings in recent times!]

What on earth were these people seeing and experiencing in the distant past? Could it be that the ancients were prone to mass hallucinations, or did they have vivid imaginations? Are all of these events only myths, legends, fantasies, or even frauds? Were all of them just flat-out crazy as they recorded this in history; ... or is there some truth to it? A lot of evidence from the ancient records indicate that the Ancients believed in a creator God. We also know from the above statements that some ancient cultures say that they have seen and talked to GOD. What else did they see, let's take a look!

Angels in Antiquity ...

The Angels flew high throughout the lofty archive of human history. The term Angel means "messenger", and they have been giving mankind their messages since time immortal. They are usually more prevalent in religion, but can be found in many cultures as "The Watchers" {or an equivalent}, giving us messages and watching over mankind; all in the service of GOD.

Throughout recorded history, writings, paintings, and statues have all been done in testimony to these Angelic messengers. What kind of information did they give to the Ancients? What types of messages are recorded for us to look at? Here are a few from the distant past to ponder!

The Roman Emperor, Constantine, said an Angel or even God himself showed him the sign of the Cross in the sky before a battle, around 300 AD, and even though the Romans were out numbered they won the fight. Did The Romans and Constantine win because of the Angelic message? Constantine believed it to be true, because soon after that event he made Christianity the religion of the Empire.

When the Temple in Jerusalem and the City were destroyed in 70 AD by the Roman army, a Roman historian, a Jewish man named Josephus recorded Angelic activity during the destuction of the Temple, and the City. The nightmarish event, according to Josephus, was that these Angels watched this historical event unfold. Would Josephus make this all up {lie}, and write it down as history, then give this to the Roman Emporer? He would only do this if he were suicidal and nuts, because if you lied in Rome you died. Josephus didn't die, so Rome believed his account of this angelic event.

Angels from heaven with a message in the sign of the cross which they gave to Constantine, and more Angels were watching as Jerusalem fell, then Josephus wrote it all down in his book "The History of the Jews". Were these two respected men from antiquity loony toons, or did they see Angels?

Next up, historical written evidence that an Angel has spoken to an Ancient; "And the Angel of the Lord called unto him {Abraham} out of Heaven". This is part of a verse from the Hebrew TORAH, (book of Genesis in the Bible, chapter 22, verse11). This is some written evidence that the ancients were spoken to by angels, according to the Torah, and the Bible.... [many theologians believe this Angel of the Lord is an appearance of Jesus Christ in the Old Testament; the term is: "theophany"]

In the message this Angel of the Lord calls to a man named Abraham, to tell him not to kill his son named Isaac, because the Lord in Heaven has ordained that through Isaac, and His son Jacob the Hebrew nation would be born ... That sounds like a pretty good message to me, the message of life from on high, from one generation to another. The message and what it accomplished was all to keep Gods plan working for the human race. Why haven't we learned this lesson of life from on high, today?

These three accounts of Angels from about 1800 BC to around 300 AD have given us a small look at some of our past. Now are these just fables, or do these accounts have wings of truth? We all know that you need wings to fly, and the Angels from antiquity are still flying today, in many faithful hearts, with a belief that these Angels are sent from God. Their thoughts are that these Angels are sent here to earth with Gods personal message for each of us. Many of the ancients also believed this to be true in their day, and we have looked at some of the written evidence for this.

Are Angels real or not? I think they are, ... so remember the next time that you are in the company of a stranger, think that you may be entertaining an Angel! ... [Or you may encounter the opposite ... a demon ...]

Demons From The Past....

Malevolent beings that have plagued mankind since the Dawn of Civilization, we call them Demons. They are the embodiment of all that is evil, [this could be the United Nations which is an un-godly entity, in my opinion], these demons oppose anything to do with good, or with God. They are a big part of our past, and according to the ancient records they are evil, deceitful, and the Bible says that they are from the dark side of reality ...

From Egypt to Babylon, through Rome and Greece these demons cast an intricate spider wed of terror in the minds, and hearts of many in the ancient world. The demons always wanted something from people, such as worship, which came in many forms. In many demon provoked rituals individuals would mutilate themselves as to appease the demons. Now; doesn't that sound like evil sadistic behavior coming from hell itself! Why would people hurt themselves for something that is not real?

In China and Australia, from Europe, and on through the Americas, demons were an infestation that they could not exterminate. All the ancient cultures of the lands mentioned above, and many more, were terrified by these evil entities. Demons could not only force people to do evil things, they could possess people and take the soul. Spooky stuff but that's what they believed and they kept a lot of records of these events. So what the hell are they?

All evidence does point to the dark side {just as the Bible has said all along}, and the abode of the dead. If you look at ancient cultures they all have a god or gods to the dead. These gods of the dead also have demon helpers, who all wreak havoc on the human race. The Egyptians have a Book of the Dead. I'll bet that book will give you nightmares!

The Druids god of the dead is called Samhain, and in days gone by he required human sacrifice during the time of year that we call Halloween. The Druids of the modern age would rather dance around Stonehenge every summer solstice, or that's what we hope they are doing!

Many people practiced animal sacrifice in their ancient rituals just to please those rulers in dark places, and these dark places exist today, just walk into the world of voodoo; and you can see it for yourself! … [Better yet just watch the Senate on C-span!]

Rituals also used to appease these gods of the dead and their demon helpers sometimes used either a virgin, or child sacrifice. One or both of these would be required, and if the sacrifice was not performed then all hell would break loose for those who disobeyed the demons. Whatever these things were most of our ancestors feared them, and sad to say killed for them. That should be proof as to what the Ancients believed when it came to demons. To them they were very real, so real that they would "kill" their own children!

THINK ABOUT THIS:

If a man or woman would kill their own children for something that modern science says exist only in the mind; then these demons that haunted the Ancients are still haunting us today. If you don't believe me, just look around for yourself. Does the word "abortion" have a haunting sound to it? Are the ancient gods of the dead behind this haunting modern ritual?

Dragons: Myth or Reality?

An object with a thirty foot wing span that has fire and smoke shooting out of it, flying through the sky and heading straight for the ground; … this must be a jet plane about to crash! Isn't it? Nope, … it's a flying, fire-breathing dragon, and the skies of antiquity are full of these ancient oddities. The ancient Chinese emperors who believed them to be "masters of the seas" and, "The Power of the Air" revered them for their power, and their ability to appear, and then disappear. Mighty dragons were magical in the Far East and were seen everywhere in the Orient, as they can be seen to this day. Just think: Chinese New Year Celebration, as their use of the dragon in this celebration is everywhere!

In this civilization that is both modern, and ancient, it amazes me that a group of people from so long ago, even unto our day could hold on to "The Power of the Air," namely the Dragon. As it was then, it remains to this day, in the skies over the Orient, the dragons are still flying! Do they fly because people have seen something, or does the power of flight come from the people's beliefs? To those of old and now, the dragons are real. We in the western world attribute this to myth, and legend; but wait a minute our Fortune cookie says: "East will meet West, when all is Dark."

In the Dark Ages in Europe,{ approximately. 500–1100 AD}, East and West did meet when dragons started flying all over Europe, and many legends, writing and drawings tell these stories of :"flying fire-breathing dragons." These are some nasty creatures, flying around setting fires to homes, castles, and even people. As they were torching everything in sight, these monsters would add misery to ma-ham, by taking a beautiful young maiden to a hidden location, never to be seen again.[where is the "Brave Heart" when you need him?]

The Knights of Medievil times were said to have fought with, and even slain these malevolent creatures. There are ancient records that say these events were taking place when the Dragons of the East traveled to the West in the times we call: "the Dark Ages." Both groups of people, in China and in Europe during the Dark Ages, believed that they saw these dragons. These two unrelated cultures in antiquity that are from different epochs and locations, both recording these strange creatures; Could they all be air-heads when it comes to the reality of fly-ing, fire-breathing dragons?

THINK ABOUT THIS:

The Dragon Poem ...
    "Myths about Dragons have come down through the ages;
You'll find them in books, just turn a few pages:
    Who is to say; if they were, ... and now are forgotten;
Only time will tell us, ... what time has left at it's bottom!"

Is the rise of the dragon in art work and decor in resent times all over America a sign that they may return soon,.. or has the clock stopped permanently for them? Well the clock is still ticking for us, so we'll just wait and see if the dragons from China and Europe fly once again! Will the modern dragons be fighter jets and bombers that fly even farther west this time?

{Mind food for thought: The Bible warns us about the Dragon, this is one of Satan's designations by GOD, we know that by reading this scripture:
    "And there appeared another wonder in heaven; and behold a great Red Dragon, having seven heads and ten horns, and seven crowns upon his head." We read this in the Bibles book of Revelation chapter 12, verse 3. This verse is about

Satan attempting to be the King of the Earth, by using the Nations of man to destroy all of Gods plan for mankind. This is my understanding of this verse, and there is a lot more of course. I just gave you a Micro. Info. Moment and I hope it leads you to read more of Gods Word on your own!}

Are the heads of the military, and a one world global community, two of the seven heads sitting on the Red Dragon, Satan, and are they about to rise here on the earth? I think they already have! Don't forget that we refer to <u>China</u> as the <u>Dragon</u>, and we use to say that <u>Russia</u> has the <u>Red Army</u>. [They still do, but we call it the Eastern Block.] Both of these areas on the earth are still communist, and these governments are the ones that hate personal freedoms for their citizens. Will someday soon the dragons of war fly, to take away "western freedoms?" The Bible says much about being aware of the Red Dragon, I think we should listen!

UFO's in Antiquity …

Are the UFO's of today in reality, the Chariots of Fire that the Bible speaks about, are angels and demons the real pilots of these mysterious "crafts?" Are the space-aliens and the gods of antiquity one and the same? Many modern theologians and book writers seem to think so. What did the Ancients think in days gone by about all of this UFO activity? You would be surprised to know that it is the same as ours in many cases.

Strange beings and their crafts are very much a part of the ancient records, in writings, and drawings, in caves and on canvas, there are paintings that depict saucer shaped crafts in the skies of the distant past. Some ancient Egyptian hieroglyphic's show depictions of what seems to be pictures of; helicopters, airplanes, and flying saucers! Was the War of the Worlds going on here on the earth before radio, and television were invented?

People all over the globe today report UFO's and alien encounters, the ancient people reported the same things, well sort of!

Let's look at an example of this which is found in the Bibles'second book of Kings. In chapter 2 verse 11 we read:

<u>"And it came to pass, as they still went on, and talked, that, behold, there appeared a Chariot of Fire, and horses of fire:, and Elijah went up by a whirlwind into heaven</u>".

Was the author of this verse mistaken when he wrote that Elijah was taken to heaven in a chariot of fire? Doesn't this sound more like a modern day flying saucer taking Elijah to outer space or at least into their craft for something?

One thing we do know from the Biblical text is that Elijah was never seen again! Is he in heaven or was he abducted by alien beings from outer space, for a medical examination? The writer of the Bible would say that he's in heaven. Where do you think Elijah went? I believe that he is in heaven, and that is a statement of my faith.

THINK ABOUT THIS:

In cave drawings that archeologists say are anywhere from 10,000 to 35,000 years old, there are depictions of what we would today call UFO's, and their occupants. If the Ancients could draw these crafts that long ago, by the time they started writing, you would think they knew the difference between flying chariots with horses of fire, and flying saucers; ... or were they that stupid? I do not believe these ancient men and women were stupid, because there are too many great works in the distant past that shows their genius status on the human intelligence scale!

[Authors side-bar: If the Chariots of Fire take people to Heaven, and the UFO's. abduct people for all kinds of weird medical examinations, give me a ticket to the Chariot, I'm out of here.]

UFO's ... Yesterday and Today ...

To many people today the interest in UFO's, the paranormal, ghosts, and things of this nature are on the rise; and they were a big part of ancient times also. I personally believe in them and I think they are the "fallen angels" written about in the first book of the Bible. In the book of Genesis chapter 6, we are given Gods reasons on why He flooded the earth in Noah's day {around 2400 BC}, and I think it shows that the "Fallen" angels were the big reason on why God did this.

[Please read chapter 6 in the Bible's book of Genesis, as the following is my view of scripture in Genesis chapter 6, coupled with my interpretation of modern UFO reports and strange paranormal activities. I believe this is all connected to the same satanic force that is found in the Bible, Gods adversary: that would be Satan, and his demonic hosts. I also think that the UFO's and the satanic demons of the Bible are one and the same. The part we shall be reading in a moment about UFO's, and demons {fallen angels} being able to manipulate matter and space-time to come into our realty for the purpose of genetically engineering a hybrid race of people; … are all also part of my conjectures on the subject. The following is my look at Genesis chap. 6, and The UFO connection of today.]

In the book of Genesis chap. 6, God destroyed all life on the earth because of mankind's violence, and also the evil thoughts of man were getting more and more wicked all the time.[does this sound like our day and age?]. But the main reason for the Flood of Noah's time was that the "fallen" angels were having sex with the daughters of Adam and Eve. By doing this they were creating a hybrid race of half man and half "fallen" angel. This was forbidden by God long ago, but these angels rebelled along with Satan and would do what they desired to, in destroying Gods salvation plan for mankind.

God destroyed the first wave of hybrids from hell in the flood, but more came after that time also. These hybrids are possibly the mighty men and women of ancient mythology, the gods of the Ancients may have been the hybrid race of giants that Satan genetically engineered here on earth. If Satan and the demons {fallen angels} can do genetic engineering of man, then they have the ability to work with materials. Such as matter, energy, sub-atomic particles; and they most likely have more technologies than we have. Don't forget we are dealing with angels here and they are evil; but they are master minds also.

If the demonic "fallen" angels of the Bible can manipulate matter and energy in the dimensions of the spirit realm, could this explain how UFO's can violate all the laws of physics? Is it possible that these evil entities have made UFO's that are of real materials that can be used and exist in all the dimensions, even the spirit realm. I think they are using the very tiny world of sub-atomic particles, and then are building, and flying these crafts that can appear and disappear in our reality. This is all accomplished by manipulating matter at the sub-atomic level, and all of this takes place in the Biblical spirit world. [This is another part my theory]

The UFO's seen today move in ways, and with speeds that would kill any living being if they were flying in one of these UFO's. If they are moving as fast as some reports have said they are {upwards of 25,000 mph have been clocked on radar}, and then these crafts are stopping completely in flight; and taking off again at high speeds. If the UFO's are traveling that quickly then stopping completely, the forces of gravity according to the laws of physics would crush the occupants in these crafts, and they would be dead. If demonic angels are piloting these UFO's from other dimensions, they wouldn't worry about death anyways; because they are already dead and in the spirit world.

So I personally think that these activities are demonic and of inter-dimensional origins. This is why these crafts and their occupants seem to "pop in" and "out" of our space-time reality: as they have been reported to do on numerous occasions. I conjecture it's because they are moving through the space-time and into our reality by traveling through other dimensions. How do they do this? Maybe they become so small in the sub-atomic world enabling these demons and their crafts to "squeeze" through the fabric of space-time. When they enter our reality by "squeezing" through the space-time dimensions these beings begin to expand and get bigger, then when they leave they get smaller to re-enter the sub-atomic realm. Is this the reason that UFO's seem to change shape, is this just the way the UFO's look when they travel through dimensions. Do ghosts and other paranormal activities have the same visual effects, I would say yes, because ghost always appear out of nowhere and return there just as fast, they are always moving in and out of are realities. I contend that this is another sign of inter dimensional space-time travel.

Most all encounters with ghosts and UFO's are very frightening to the individuals, and this sounds like demonic activities to me. People are not seeing or experiencing the friendly "ghost" of a loved one, or our kindly "space-brothers" here to help, no most of these events "scare" these people half to death!. So I believe all arrows point to demonic beings hell bent on harming us, and hell bound in their eternal destination. These evil entities are always trying to take us with them to the "PIT," … so beware of them.

Do these alien beings do any good for mankind now or in the past? It doesn't seem that way if we look at the mass majority of UFO abductions in recent times. What we find is that most people feel an evil presence, and a sensation of lost time, almost as if they are in another dimension. The alien abductors also do all kinds of medical procedures. Many people that have been abducted say they have had reproductive experiments done, only to be re-abducted latter and then shown a hybrid humanoid child. Now does this sound like the same thing that Satan and the fallen demonic angels did in Genesis chap. 6,[genetic engineering], because that's what it sounds like to me. I and the Ancients agree that UFO's, and all of this evil stuff are real. This activity has gone on in the distant past and this activity is still going on in our day.

Think About This:

In modern UFO research it seems the space aliens always find there way into the lives of people who have recently been involved with the occult; does the darkness arrive when man invites it in? Are the UFO's really of satanic origin?

I will say yes they are of evil origins, because of all the abduction cases investigated there has never been a real Bible believing Christian taken on board a UFO. To avoid abduction they have spoken the name, Jesus Christ, because their faith is in Him!

The aliens either don't like His name or they are in fear of the Lord, I think they are afraid of a man named Jesus Christ.

Why would intelligent beings from outer-space be in fear of a mortal man? They would only be afraid if the man was God, and the aliens were demons though!

Ancient Power Stations in the Pyramids and more ...

What if I told you that in the not so distant past our planet had only one giant continent ... Would you believe me? Well don't, just look at the globe and see how the eastern coasts of the Americas fit together with the western shorelines of Africa and Europe just like a giant jig-saw puzzle. Coincidence, guess again. In modern plate-tectonics, [the study of movements in the earths crust], many geologists are also sure that the earth had one single land mass millions, or possibly even just a few thousand years ago.

Try to picture in your minds eye all seven continents as one, with the geometric center located in the Middle East of our day, the area that we call the Cradle of Civilization, a place the Bible says is the Garden of Eden. Was the lost civilization of Atlantis, west of Eden on this one giant continent? Then as this one continent broke apart with plate tectonics, was Atlantis consumed by the Atlantic Ocean with most of the real tangible evidence for their existence lost, or did some of their knowledge and technology survive on each side of the Atlantic Ocean? Is the evidence from Atlantis, and possibly from the Garden of Eden, all in the pyramids?

On five of the seven continents of today, we find pyramids or giant mounds that are shaped like pyramids. Why are they all over the earth, and why this shape? Is there more to these than meets the eye? We still use them today, they are on our dollar bill, also at the Lou've in France there is a giant glass pyramid, and there is even one in Memphis, TN ... maybe this one was for Elvis! Some people today claim pyramids have strange powers that radiate from them. Do they have strange powers or could they even be ancient power stations? Are the pyramids remnants of power stations from Atlantis, or maybe even the technology learned from the Garden of Eden?

In a place called Giza in Egypt stands the Great pyramid, one of the seven wonders of the ancient world. Most Egyptologists believe that the Pyramid was built as a tomb for the Pharaoh Kufu, strange thing is that the only evidence is a three inch statue of Kufu as proof, and this was found miles away from the pyramid. There are no hieroglyphics inside, or on the outside, to tell us who it was built for. There were never any artifacts, or even a mummy found inside. So was it really a tomb?

Now if the Eygptians didn't build it as a tomb, then who built it and why? The Cradle of Life is still rocking out the questions after all these years, isn't it! What then is this astrological and mathematically precise stucture anyway? Let me try to explain my idea of what they were.

First, the Earth is a giant spinning electric motor that generates electricity, think lightning. Secondly, the Earth also has an electro-magnetic field that could produce levitation, think about the way two magnets repel each other. Thirdly, the Earth has Energy Ley-Lines that have very high concentrations of this energy from the electro-magnetic field. These energy ley-lines seem to run through many of the ancient structures, such as: the Great Pyramid in Egypt, Stonehenge on the Salisbury Plain, the Mayan Temples here in the Americas, and possibly even many others. These ley-lines may have acted just like our modern day electrical power grids!

An ancient power grid of ley-lines may have been used as under ground conduits for energy and electro-magnetism. This energy could then be transferred from one ancient power station to another to use as levitation devices. This may be how they could move blocks hundreds of miles weighing as much as, anywhere from four to four hundred tons, or even more. By moving these mammoth stones with levitation, sometimes from hundreds of miles away, the ancients could then use this building materiel for these massive structures in antiquity. [To this day no one really knows how they built all these ancient structures, and levitation devices are my conjecture only]

[Mind food for thought: In an area close to Stonehenge there is a massive copper mine that is thousands of years old, but is not in use today. Is this location just a coincidence, or is this an ancient electrical cable? Take into account that we use copper as a way to send electricity today, from point A to B!]

Did the Ancients power up the planet, even before Franklin discovered electricity while flying his kite? Were the Ancients using this electricity in combination with precious gems and crystals to create laser beams for cutting stones so precisely that we can't repoduce this today with our modern technology? Did the Ancients direct high powered electricity through crystals to create a laser beam so powerful that it could "cut" stones with 100% measurement accuracy? The building stones in the Great Pyramid, Mayan Temples, and many others, are cut so precisely that a dollar bill will not fit in between the seams of these building stones: some weighing as much as a 747 Jet!

[Micro Info. Moment: Modern history books tell us that this work was done by our primitive ancestors with pick axes, chisels, and man power. This is possible, but not probable. It may be more like laser beam cutting devices and levitation from The Atlantis Power Co.]

With the Earth as one giant continent, and the main power station located where Atlantis was thought to be, namely the Atlantic Ocean, with under ground cables, that we call energy ley-lines, transferring energy to other stations known today as: Stonehenge, the Great Pyramid, Mayan Temples, and maybe even the Temple Mount in Jerusalem. Did the main power station in Atlantis blow-up and shut down all the others, thus ending mankind's second epoch on Earth? {The first epoch being Eden} Did mans first chance after the Garden of Eden, all go up in smoke?

The Great Pyramid A Masterpiece In Stone

Let us look at the Great Pyramid, is it just an enigma in time, or was it the main power station on the ancient earth, after Atlantis was lost? Was it built as a tomb for the dead or for energy, power, and life for the living? Remember no mummy or artifacts, ect ..., have ever been found, inside!

What we do know about The Pyramid is this: it is definitely an astrological observatory for a look at the galactic picture, with mathematics incorporated into the design that we have only rediscovered in modern times. It was built so precisely, that it has moved only one half of an inch in all these thousands of years! Today things fall apart in a week.

With their star gazing capabilities, and their understandings of complicated mathematics, the builders of the Great Pyramid could have easily tapped into the Earths electro-magnetic energies for all kinds of usage.

As I stated previously the energy could have been used for laser-beam cutting devices, and for levitation to transport mammoth building materials great distances. Did these ancient ones also use this levitation for flying vehicles on the planet, even before we could drive? If they could fly, then how did they do it?

Invisible lines of power are all around the earth, some work as a cushion and can hold visible objects in the air. Did the Pyramid generate this energy to fly vehicles? There are Egyptian hieroglyphics that do seem to indicate that the Ancient Ones were in the air, even before the Wright Bro's first manned flight in an airplane.

THINK ABOUT THIS:

We use high voltage electrical power to generate magnetic levitation for moving high speed trains on tracts { these trains are called Mag-lev high speed Bullet trains}, what if the Ancients could have harnessed the massive electro-magnetic powers of the Earth for use in propelling vehicles in the air, how fast could they go? Could they go into space, or could they go into other dimensions? Only the Ancients can answer these questions, we can only speculate, just as I have here.

We use high powered lasers for cutting in modern times that can not reproduce cutting techniques that the Ancients seem to have had. Did you know that in Central America five perfectly cut crystal human skulls have been found that look as if they were cut by lasers! Yet these "skulls" are at least hundreds and possibly even thousands of years old! Were these "skulls" cut in Atlantis with ancient lasers, with the original knowledge coming from Eden?

Were the Great Pyramid, Stonehenge, Mayan Temples, and other ancient monuments constructed by laser-beams and levitation from the earth itself, was there power to light up the Earth here before Edison invented the light bulb? Only the builders can answer those questions, and I will ask this: "Do the pyramids on the earth today hold the answers to all of our energy needs in this modern age?" A theoretical possibility would be to generate a high concentration of electro-magnetism through one of these Ancient monuments and see what happens!

Were these ancient monuments built as tombs for death, or were they constructed for life, and the living? My theory would say that they were built and used for life. When the Earth was one giant continent did the descendants of the Biblical Garden build the civilization of Atlantis? Did they also bring technology with them that we only dream of as being in the future? Had these master scientists of antiquity been given information, from on High, on how to harness the powers of the Earth, and Space? Is that why they were so precise in calculating movements in the heavens, as to collect this natural energy and store it in the pyramids for usage when needed? To me all the above are closer to the truth than what I was taught in public school, and by the scientific community through my own research.

We today marvel and wonder about places such as the Great Pyramid, and Stonehenge … yet we call these ancient builders primitive, even though we do not really know who, how, or why the Ancients built these magnificent monuments in antiquity. We do know that they were always watching the skies and counting with mathematical precision as the time passes in the universe. Who were these Ancients that had this knowledge at the beginning of recorded history, were they just cavemen growing smarter, or did they have the knowledge all along from on High? Do all the ancient monuments on earth have ties to the Biblical Garden of Eden?

You decide the answers as you ponder this old Proverb from the Bible: [Prov.25:2]
"It is the glory of God to conceal a thing: but the honor of kings is to search out a matter."

As we search, do we find the hidden things of God and become royalty in glory, or do we never even try to look? The Ancients star gazers were always looking at the beauty of the universe and searching out the glory of God; … we would be wise to follow their example! Do you follow GOD, or do you follow everything that modern science tells us?

As we have moved in time from the Garden of Eden, through Atlantis, then on to the ancient power stations in the pyramids are you looking at history a little bit differently? If not then lets keep walking through the corridors of time.

The Greeks And The Romans:

All over Europe, Asia, and the Middle East we find remnants, and records, from the Greeks and the Romans. These two ancient civilizations still influence our western society to this day. The Greeks would seek out reason, purpose, and knowledge, as opposed to the Romans who sought conquest, and a one world empire. From about 500 B.C., to around 400 A.D., both of these ancient super powers had world dominance at one time, first the Greeks, and then the Romans.

As these two Empires marched in the distant past, they are still marching on in our modern times, with their ways of government, laws, and architecture. A lot of the government buildings in the U.S.A. have some Greek, and Roman style architecture with columns, arches, and vaulted ceilings over head. Our laws are made in, and the government is run out of Greek and Roman style buildings.

So apparently we take these guys very seriously when it comes to things such as government, our laws, even architecture. In reality how do we feel about them when it comes to things like God, or the gods, how seriously do we take them? When these guys had more gods running around in togas, than a college dorm party! Did they believe in these creators of life, or were they all superstitious dumb bells stumbling their way around in a god induced stupor?

The gods to these people were very real, and played in a big part of their lives. That is why they built so many grand temples to them in both of these Empires. The Greeks and Romans worshiped many gods, and both had a god of war. Mars was the Roman god of war and Zeus was the Greeks. From Greek philosophers to Roman Emperors the gods were on the minds, and in the hearts of them all.

The Greeks built magnificent structures with their understanding of design and mathematics, while the Romans mastered roads, and water ways, namely the Aqueducts. These ancient ruins are still here with us today to marvel at, and to this day we do not completely understand the technologies they used; for some of the things they accomplished.

One of these is the coliseum in Rome which was a public blood fest of slaughter and death, … nice building but I wouldn't want a ticket! The Roman Empire was a war machine, of killing, and conquering, then taxes, and a one world order, [you see the new world order is not new, it's just being repackaged].

The Roman god of war, Mars, was a big part of their belief system. Did the god of war say that public blood fests were alright? The answer apparently is yes, as history shows us that the Roman Empire ended in a blood-fest by the barbarians from the north.

As the old saying goes, "To live by the sword, is to die by the sword". Rome was living by war and died by the same. With all their skills in other areas they just had to keep on fighting, man never learns. Does he?

THINK ABOUT THIS:

If the gods of war that live in mythology are real only in the minds of our ancestors, why is there war all over the planet in 2007, have we taken more from the Greeks, and Romans than we think? Are Mars, and Zeus, the gods of War; still with us in our modern age? You decide!

The Greeks, Did They Think Too Much?

Athens, Greece, the Seat of Thought in the ancient world, men of the mind, the original "think tank"; What was on their minds? It sure wasn't the stock market or commodities; these guys were deep thinkers about the workings of man in the universe. How they relate to each other and why, and who, or what made every thing. These philosopher's and wise men, knew about the atom before we made the "bomb." The Greeks had tragedies and talk sessions well before modern psychology came into being, you see they were all about the mind; … because there had to be an explanation for everything. Was the explanation, a God, or did "matter" just appear as a by-product of the universe? These were some of the questions the Greeks were asking and pondering, in so many eons past.

Zeus, Apollo, and Hercules, were gods of the Greeks but they did not have a god for "everything". They did have a god of "The Unknown", we know of this because in the Bibles' New Testament, Paul address' the Greek philosophers at "Mars Hill" in Greece, (Oh no, there is the war god, Mars, again!) Paul asked them this question: "I see that you have here an alter to The Unknown God; with your devotions, do you worship Him?", so Paul deduced that the Greeks worshiped the Unknown God; … and we can also infer this by the question he asked.

Did worshiping the Unknown God on Mars Hill lead the Greeks down the road of the unthinkable; and does this road lead to a dead-end? The road that the Greeks took led them into the "War-Zone" as they were conquered by the Romans, in of course war!

In all their building talents, and at all of their genius, we look back in awe at what the Greeks and Romans did in the nine hundred or so years of the time that these two Empires ruled the world. Two Empires crumpled in time by war, but they are still very much a part of the western ways of life: in our laws and forms of government, architectural styles, and much of our way of thinking, you see Rome and Greece live on with us today! It seems that their gods of war have prevailed into our time, also!

The Scale of Intelligence …

As the time has passed on planet Earth, from Babylon, to Egypt, through Greece, Rome, and civilizations that are lost in the very distant past, all of them have contributed something for our present. We in the modern age look back at these Ancient Ones with awe and wonderment, because they were masters of the skies with their knowledge of astronomy, and they were masters of the Earth, with their mathematical brilliance. These people were highly educated scientists with insights that we are only rediscovering in our computer induced age of high "tech" ... so we have a lot of nerve calling them "primitive ape men". These men, and women, the <u>first Adams</u> and <u>Eves</u>, were <u>geniuses</u> on the historical stage of life, and on the <u>scale of human intelligence</u>!

We are told that the human race is advancing, then how could we go from the Age of Brilliance in 4000 B.C., to the "Dark Ages" in 1000 A.D.? From smart to dumb, did we go backwards? At one point in history we did go backwards but now we are in the up turn because from the historical record it seems we are on the rise in intelligence once again starting in about 1500 A.D., with the Renaissance in Europe. This rekindled the fire that sparked the Industrial Revolution of the 1800s', which has brought us to our Modern High-Tech Computer Age, here in 2007.

Our human time line seems to start on a high point, then move to a low point, and now we are moving back up. This would seem to indicate a human history with peaks and valleys, rather than a steady Ascent of Man, as modern evolution would like us to believe. While the Bible says we are a fallen race that will have high and low points.

Evolution states that: mankind is advancing, the Bible says that: the human race will always be the same. The Bible is "predictive", while evolution science is in "theory."

If we are advancing as a species, why do our three basic human feelings stay the same? Our <u>human emotions</u>, <u>thoughts</u>, and <u>experiences</u> do not change with the passing of time, we seem to be the same as the clock tic's on.

The human <u>emotions</u> of, loving, or hating, laughing, or crying, a feeling of being "on top of the world" or the feeling of "crawling under a rock", due to embarrassment, every peason ever born has felt some of these emotions, right! Unless of course you are Mr. or Mrs. Ice-Cube!

The <u>thoughts</u> of man, have these changed over time? Well today as it was yesterday, we as people still think a lot about God, and or personal gods that some people worship. All over the earth and in outer space we study the heavens like the Ancients did; we are all fascinated by the night sky! Our high tech. modern age of computers is done all by mathematical equations, just as our ancestors before studied Math, all of us throughout time think about solving the problems. We think about families and friends, our health, the good times, and the bad times of our lives, and at times we ponder our deaths.

Throughout history these are the very similar thoughts that men and women in any time of history have, all of us at one moment or another. You and I are more alike than we are different, and it doesn't matter how different we may seem in appearance, we are alike inside; … just as the Bible predicted.

Our human <u>Experience</u>, has this changed as time has moved forward? The answer from antiquity through our day is … NO! Just look around for yourself as the human experience is everywhere, so go out and interact with other people, which is the "Human Experience!" To enjoy one another from the Love of God, that is a True Human Experience. Listen to your heart sometimes and follow Gods lead, then you are on the Eternal Experience, and it doesn't get any better!

Are the Mind, Soul, and Spirit of man any different today as that of the Ancients? The historical records say, No; but we today, say that we have changed because of our technology. If this is true, is it for the better, or for the worse? The Present holds the answer to that question.

As for us, we move on into the Present, because "Clock Number One", the Past has now, Tic, tic, tic … Stopped!

Chapter Two

Clock Two: The Present ... tic, tic, tic ...
Where are we now?

The Age of Modern Man Begins.

The mind of man was experiencing an almost endless flow of genius in the Age of Discovery, between the mid 1800's through the mid twentieth century. If only they knew where these discoveries would take us! Insight, inventions, discoveries in science, and medicine, with a look into the very tiny world of the "atoms," the discoveries from the mind of man; ... so very many that they made and used. Into the cosmos they peered with giant new telescopes, studying the heavens as never before, from gamma-rays, to radio-waves, the Periodic Table of Elements, and the electricity to power up the earth. All of these were a product of this explosion in human ingenuity; mankind's rise from the Middle-Ages was now nearing the summit!

Mathematics took a giant leap forward, and so did mankind in 1969 when Neil Armstrong stepped onto the moon. Building engineering took us to the next level, with the invention of structural steel, we were able to calculate the answers to problems as never before, and build things stronger, longer, and higher than anything that had been built on the planet in the past. So it seems these guys, and gals, picked a lot of knowledge from the time tree of life!

This time period of history is so rich with discoveries that have made possible many modern conveniences that the inventors themselves could only dream about. The good Dr Einstein whose insights made space travel a reality, never flew in space. He only dreamed we could, their dreams became our realities. What are we doing with these dreams that are now the realities we live in? As the human race continues, how close to the finish line are we? When we now know that the Middle Ages are over, and our technologies have moved us to the summit of our knowledge. Will we out smart ourselves before we finish the race, or ever reach the top of the mountain? One thing that we do know is that the Present clock is running right now, and you and I are in it … Tic … Tic … Tic

The Modern Civil Society: Oh, is it Really?

Beep, # beep,* Ring, *ring, ring*, Lights Flashing! ^!, Bells*#, and Whistles-@!!@ going off, PIN numbers going in 3-2-1, with $ CASH coming out. With all of the Noise and Action going on, is this a slot machine at Las Vegas sounding off the Jack Pot, or a pinball machine that's about to TILT? How about a child's video game blowing up everything in the world? All with very Real LOUD Exploding sounds that emanate from it!

All of the above, and much, much, more, this is our modern society all around the globe; with all of the Noise; the air-waves are full on the "Boom-Box" in space. Everywhere we go you can hear every imaginable sound that is coming out of every imaginable thing!! There are cell-phones "ringing-out" more songs than the radio, planes are flying over head, cars, trucks, and trains moving to and fro all over the Earth today; all contributing to the "noise pollution!" Car alarms tell people to "Stay away from the vehicle," while computer automated answering machines tell us to "Push # 1: for assistance, push # 2: for info. push # 3: for help, by the time you get to "push # 4" all you want to do is push the OFF button on them, so we hang-up, all TIC-ED-OFF! Frustration, noise, and a fast pace of life are in almost every culture and society on the planet in 2007, and sorry to say that my society in the West is leading the race, with the East not that far behind. Mankind is now always in a race, or in a hurry all the time, in this modern "Age of Speed!"

Does it make any sense to rush your own life when life moves quickly on its own, but our modern society pushes us for more and more speed?

Are we more civil now in the fast track society, or do we lose intimacy? Do we YELL all the time to be heard over all the Noise of Planet Earth a giant "Boom-Box" in space! Are we losing touch with each other; while the Pace of Life accelerates, exponentially?

I would give you an answer to all of this; but I have to take my Cell-Phone Call … and while you wait …

THINK ABOUT THIS:

We have all kinds of information at our fingers tips with the internet, right, yet this generation is so uninformed, and by being uninformed, this will always lead to an ignorance in the general population of a society. Is this why the U.S.A has had a steady drop in overall IQ's in the population over the last 30 years? [This is a by-product of public schools in my honest opinion] In this age of communication, with the inter-net, cell-phones, and e-mail, is all the technology a big reason why the art of the spoken word is being lost? [Just think T-E-X-T—M-E-S-S-A-G-E- … the new cell-phone language, only letters and "codes" … no real words … strange but true in our day]

With out face to face communication, something gets lost in the real communication between people, and with out this communication, what are we as a civil society?

[Mind food for thought: When governments can keep its citizens from communicating with each other face to face, watch your backs because; that is called social engineering]

The inventors of the television in the 1950's never even saw a cable program, were they missing anything that is enlightening us today here in 2007? It doesn't look that way, because people in general spend more time today with machines than any group of people in the history of mankind. More time is spent with machines of one type or another and less time is being spent with each other. Is that good for society? I don't think it is!

Here is a small list of machines that we use and spend a lot of time with: driving or riding in cars, busses, trains, and on bicycles, we spend hours a day interacting with a computer, or watching TV, talking on your cell-phone, operating the washer and dryer, cooking in the Micro-wave, elevators going up and down sky-scrapers, air-planes flying us everywhere, ATM's handing out cash, we go from self check-out counters, to pumping our own gas. The Machines are everywhere, and the list goes on, and on and on, as they take up more and more of our time. My advice is drop the machines for a short time and just go for a walk, or find a quiet place to sit, and then enjoy the moments of "peace" and "quiet", then be thankful that you have life! [Just as our grandparents and parents told us that life is a gift from God, so be good and be thankful]

Two of the great things about our ancestors of the last generation, {those born in the 1920's and 30's}, is that they never missed a good conversation <u>face</u> to <u>face</u>, and they were brave enough to fight communism and fascism. Will we fight this war again here on our own soil? I would say we are doing that right now and that is why there are many new "freedom" movements gaining new people all the time, Americans are fed up with the Fed, Period.[one of these freedom movements is; www. info wars.com, on the inter-net, and it's free.]

[Don't forget that control freaks always keep people from talking to each other. Sound something like a communist plot unfolding, well it should because; it may be happening right now with all the new spying going on by our own government, on it's own citizens. My recommendation is: watch what you do on your computer and Beware of the Cameras and Micro-phones being installed in cities all over the U.S.A., with all the governmental spying it doesn't sound like America to me. Our individual part of the battle is to keep talking to God and your most trusting family members, friends and fellow Americans who understand the Constitution. For it is "we the people" who are the real America under God, it's not the government with their new computers, and spying methods, never was and please don't forget that!]

Is evidence stating to show us that a <u>New World Order</u> is conditioning people with technologies that keep us away from each other and persuade us to trust in the "system" more? I personally see it happening and in my opinion, from being an observer of our <u>social degeneration</u> in the last 25 years, people seem more easily led astray with governmental liars! Two examples are President Clinton when he lied about his adulterous affair and also President Bush lying about weapons of mass destruction. One is a Democrat the other is a Republican and they think that they are gods of the age, as they can do and say anything they want. Bottom line is they lie from the top office in the country, getting away with it, and they don't care what "we the people" think. This is already a form of "mind control," by conditioning people to except liars as leaders. We have it all backwards today, … do we not? Watching more and more ungrateful liars saying they are looking out for us, I Don't Think So! This is all just a testimony to a <u>selfish pride</u> that has <u>infected our leaders</u>.

I also think we are trusting on the computer way too much {this is what the controllers want us to do}, and in the not to distant future we may pay a high price tag for this fast dance with technology. Only time will tell if that will come true!

The Computer … Beep … Beep … A King …

"Silicon sequence My lights start to flash; exotic equations those are my task;

I've made life so easy for man; but do they know who, I Really Am;

Made here on Earth to help you along; you wrote the tune, but I stole the song;

"Beep, Beep, Beep, I'm the King of the world, and it's you, you, you! That I have fooled."

Here a computer, there a computer, Whoops, I should have said "everywhere there's a computer." In the last ten years computers have become such an integrated part of our every day activities that we today have become at least fifty percent dependent on them, or more. They are in hospitals to monitor life, the traffic lights are computerized, and we have robots that are made by other robots, while the air traffic around the globe is all in their control. School children as young as five can use them, and Grams and Gramps can log-on to the Net. It seems that everyone is using this wonder of the age.

There are satellites with silicon brains that watch us here on the Earth. You can even be located anywhere on the planet, by the Global Positioning System {GPS}, using the micro-chip in your cell phone. Modern communication, and travel on land, sea, and air, would come to a halt, and so would our modern society if the computers all shut down. If the computers shut down in the U.S.A so does all commerce; because our entire over the road trucking of goods is all "computerized" today! <u>No travel, no food, no food and we strave to death</u>. Easy equation isn't it.

[my advice is to stock up on at least a 2 month supply of can goods and nonperishables, with a bunch of bottled water, and an alternative power source; cause you never know do ya'!]

THINK ABOUT THIS:

If computers shut down all travel so that food could not be shipped, and millions of people starve to death, would it be the computers fault or ours? The answer to that is becoming more difficult because we are creating computers that can think on their own. The next question is, will the computers shut us off of our own food supply and other modern life essentials?

Keep in mind that after the Y2K non-event with the computer date roll-over, from 1999 to 2000, where the only thing that occurred was, the governments of the world had all the computers on the earth hooked together in one or two central data-bases. One is in the USA, and the other is probably in Europe. So theoretically thinking all the computers could communicate with each other, and that could have devastating consequences for the human race in the near future.

Artificial Intelligence … The Mind Man Has Made …

The "artificial mind" that man has created is all over the place, from the simplist talking doll, to the most the complicated voice interactive computers. They can talk, and walk and we are making them to think on their own. These creations of man already moniter a big part of our daily lives, will one day in the future history say this about us?

"In the silicon valley men went in: but in the end, out of the valley walked the Silocon Men".

With robots and computers doing so much of everything today are we giving up a big part of our <u>human experience</u> to these machines, as they take on more, and more of our daily tasks. Have these machines become our security blankets? Oh no, blankets are for small children and we're all grown up in 2007, aren't we, … or have we become like a rebellious "teen-age" society where we always want more, and more of what we really don't need? These minds that man has made are robbing many people of the human experience, as mankind goes deeper into the land of artificial intelligence, to a place called cyber-space!

The Land of Cyber-OZ … a bedtime story for adults …

In cyber-space you can create your own realities; you can even create a new identity, and even a real "cool" personality! As people float around in Cyber-space, half person/half machine, tethered to their computers like an astronaut in space; do they realize where they are? When people spend hours "Surfing the web", just for something to do, they must beware of the spider that made the web in the first place. This spider may catch you in the web and devour your experiences with other real people, in real time, in person.

Real people do not hide in what can be the make believe of Cyber-space where hearts, minds, and courage, come from Cyber-Oz. In the Wizard of Oz who was behind the curtain? It sure wasn't the Wizard! Behind the workings of Cyber-space, and the Web, are wires, no Wizard either, just wires! The End!

By this point you could conclude that I have something against all of this technology, well I don't! There are many wonderfull applications of computers, robotics, and the inter-net in our society in 2007. Then again on the other side of this two edged sword, we call modern technology, lets hope we don't cut off more than we can chew, least in the near future we will have to eat it and choke to death as a race of people.

As time goes on will the computer be mans best friend or the ultimate enemy of man? Will the robots we make today, rule us in the future with the intelligence we programmed into them? In a virtual reality world will we love fantasies, more than each other, will a machine without a heart, steal the heart of mankind, will we become the Tin-man of Oz, a robot ourselves, in need of a new heart?

The super computers we have today blow our minds at how fast they can do things, one of these even beat the best player in the world at Chess, the game of war strategies. The military programs computers all the time for war related activities, will the computers use their intelligence of warfare, to wage war on us, and who would win? Well, they beat us in Chess, haven't they?

Man's Mind and Hands … Making all this "Stuff"….

Discoveries, inventions, innovations, our dreams and ideas that are made into realities here in 2007; the Mind with the Hands of man keeps-on giving us more, and more "Stuff." In our western society, and moving quickly around the globe, every convenience thought possible is made possible, the "stuff" of "science fiction" just fifty years ago sits in our family rooms today; one is the "plasma TV", and we all know there are hundreds of others! We can fly anywhere in the world in a days travel, or we can go anywhere on the Earth with a "virtual reality head set", and never have to leave our house! We can work from our homes on computers, or we can commute there on under ground subway systems. Cooking dinner is a thing of the past for most people today, "Take-Out" or, "Nuke-It", is the way we get our main course, and the only dinner bells we hear are the door bell, and the micro-wave! You can do your own laundry at home on machines with more settings than the Space-Shuttle, or just drop it off at the cleaners for pick up later. Shopping can be done for anything, at anytime of day or night in our 24-7 society.

Cable TV has given us unlimited entertainment choices, cell-phones allow us to communicate with anybody, at anyplace, and at anytime. The world wide "Web"gives us the abilities to access all kinds of information, while "cyber-space" allows us to become anyone we want to be, all this "Stuff" for our convenience, ease, and fun! Many people think that all of this "Stuff" is great, and yes some of it is, … but let's ask ourselves a needed question: "is all this "stuff" really necessary?"

THINK ABOUT THIS:

Here is an old saying; that I just made up: "If you over stuff a turkey it will not cook properly, it will burn. With all of our "Stuff," are we the turkey? Will we burn ourselves someday in the Nuclear War Oven?"

Maybe we should stop over stuffing ourselves with all this needless "junk" and listen to Grandma, who always said: "You have to cook the Thanksgiving turkey slow and don't <u>over stuff</u> it or it will <u>burn!</u>"

Do people need every "Gadget" on the planet in their everyday lives? The answer would most likely be, ... No! Can we help stop the turkey, that's US, from being toasted by the "nuclear oven", ... yes we can, by first understanding that you and I are "wonderfully "made" as individuals with certain gifts from God. Once you understand that we all have a higher purpose in eternity most fears and anxieties will dissipate; because once you start to understand God's truth, then you are on God's side, and He is on your side. Simple stuff for the simple as sheep people, and that my friend is us; ... yes you, and I at times, ... are simple as sheep! [That is why we need a "good shepherd;" which is one of Jesus Christ's titles in the Bible, is this a coincidence ... I don't think so!]

Here is God's truth about how you, and I have been made by GOD's heavenly "Stuff:"

"<u>I am fearfully and wonderfully made: When I was made in secret ... your eyes {the Lords} did see my substance {DNA?} Yet being imperfect in thy book all my members {our bodies} were written ... which were fashioned {God made us}.... How precious are your thoughts unto me, O God!</u>" [Partial verses from the book of Psalms in the Old Testament, chapter 139: verses 13 thru 17]

I believe these statements say that we are made by God in a "miraculous" way. Now let's take a look at how "wonderfully" we are made!

The Master Piece of GOD ... Man and Woman ...

What modern medicine knows about the brain can blow your mind, and what they don't know is driving them crazy! Our brains on average weigh about three pounds, and are approximately four by six inches in size, so they are not very big, and they weigh very little. The amazing thing is that this "gray matter" the brain, is the most complex thing in the known universe, and the mind of man is trying to figure out the workings of the organ that is producing our thoughts! And they still do not fully understand how it works. Who would have thought that, lets say brain teaser now!

Today with modern neurology, we know that the brain is a compelx super computer that runs on electrical impulses, a miraculous piece of equipment in the mechanics of life. Our brains are actually pre-coded to run the body that contains it, that in its own right is strange. What came first the body or the brain; they both need each other to work, do they not?

Electrical signals traveling though miles of wires, called our nervous system, sending signals back and forth from the central control center, the brain. These signals are sending information to everybody system and function, with instructions on how to work. The pullies, cables, and the hydraulic system; ... read those as the muscles, joints, ligaments, and tendons. Also inside of us we have the bones which are the structural steel that supports our bodies. Inside of the body we find a massive filtration system with the liver, kidneys, spleen, and the pancreas. The energy from our food and drink is made inside our nuclear reactor, called the digestive tract, then what isn't needed is sent on to waste management for disposal. The Heart is the master pump for the "river of life", our blood, sending oxygen and nutrients throughout the body to keep us alive!

What an amazing array of specialized organs and complicated systems that is inside this miracle machine of life, that we call the human body. Electrical signals sending information with miles of wires, hydraulic motors, filtration systems, and pumping stations where valves open and close all for the liquid fuel that runs the whole system. Is this a modern factory, or a machine?

It is a machine of sorts, because it is just as complicated as a computerized modern machine. Isn't it? This is the machine of life, a miracle we call the human body, that's all controlled by the brain, in a pre-coded message, from the computer in our head!

[Authors side bar: We know that there are pre-coded messages in our brains to control our bodies. Are there more codes and who coded them in the first place?]

DNA The Living Code....

The building blocks of life are a pre-coded set of instructions that tell us who we will be as a person, even before we are born. This information is all in the DNA Code that we receive from our parents. These instructions are in the smallest "How To" manual on the planet, which is in our DNA. The DNA molecule has stumped molecular biologists because of the intricate design in its structure and in the complex way it uses to manufacture the living cell. These tiny cells are in reality "living factories" with "miniature machines" that operate in similar fashion to our machines and factories. So who's copying who here, God or man? In other words the tiny cell operates like a complex factory, just like the ones we build. Once again; are we duplicating the plan, … or do we build factories because it is already coded into the way we work also? Is this another code from the Creator?

The DNA molecule is a small alphabet "code" of four letters {a, c, g, t, these are their scientific designations}, and there are "billions" of code combinations that are in the DNA. The DNA is the library of information in the nucleus of the cell that gives instructions to the RNA molecule. The RNA takes the instructions to another part of the cell to start assembling some of the 20 different amino acids that in turn make the proteins, some 30,000 of them!

With some 30,000 proteins, 20 different amino acids, and 4 DNA letters, by just looking at the numbers involved to make just one living cell, we see a level of coding inside the "factories" of life. This shows me that the living cell is very precise and mathematical in the organization of the cells composition, rather than a random chance "dice-game"; read that evolution.

The following is my simplified version of the makings of a living cell. See if it seems like "random chance" or by "intelligent design"! First living cells need to come from other living cells; that are procreating, life from life.

After conception the cells start to from and now the DNA molecule goes to work. First the DNA library give instructions to the RNA shuttle bus, which goes to the Amino Acids warehouse to pick up the supplies to build Proteins for the Living Cell factories.

Number <u>one</u> is <u>procreation</u>, <u>second</u> is the <u>DNA</u>, <u>third</u> the <u>RNA</u>, <u>fourth</u> are the <u>amino acids</u>, <u>fifth</u> would be the <u>proteins</u> and the <u>sixth</u> is the <u>living cell</u>.

Let's look at the numbers in the "Code,": There are <u>6</u> levels of the cell development as we saw above, then we have the <u>4</u> letters in the DNA, plus the <u>20</u> amino acids and the <u>30,000</u> proteins; … that's a lot of numbers if you start adding them up. With all the numbers there are billions of "code combinations" to choose from here. Can a cosmic accident organize all of the different "code combinations?" I mean can random chance do all this assembling in factory precision with all of the steps involved in creating a living cell. I don't believe that a cosmic accident can organize anything. That's way we call it an "accident", it's not suppose to occur!

The DNA molecule shows me evidence of design in the fabric of every living thing on planet Earth. It is as though even the "living cells" are communicating on the information highway that travels through our bodies and keeps us alive; on the road of the "Living Cell."

What makes the DNA cars run [communicate], on this highway that produces the living cell? Science doesn't really know the answer; all they know is that they can't drive there just yet! [Figure-out how the living cell is made by the proteins that are "talked" to by the DNA!]

THINK ABOUT THIS:

The DNA molecule is a small alphebetical code of four letters in combination with twenty amino acids that make up all the thousands of proteins, which in turn make the living cells. How do the non-thinking molecules know which letters to pick? What, or who is telling them? Is it random chance on the letter choice, or is there a code built in that has pre-selected the letters already! Ah! We see the mathematics of life in the cell itself; everything has a count to it in nature. Such as seven colors in the rainbow, to the billons upon billons of stars in the universe, and even the DNA molecule has a count. If everything in nature has a count to it, the question is; "Is there a master counter", and if so, could the Master count the billion upon billions of stars?

In the Old Testament Book of Psalms, 147:4, we read this: "<u>The LORD counted the number of stars; He calls them by their names</u>".

Is this designer and counter of the stars counting DNA letters also? Is there an Intelligent Designer behind the "Curtain of Life" or is it just Random Choice … I pick the first … how about you?

The Mind of Man … Who Do We Think We Are?

Today we understand that our brains are pre-wired with billons of nerve-endings, and neurons that run our bodies and our minds. These thoughts in the mind of man are they just random electrical impulses from chemical inter-actions, in the organ we call; the brain? Can a mass of living cells cause us to think, and what is it; that causes this "spark of thought" in each of us anyway?

Our sensory perceptions like: sight, sound, touch, smell, and taste are all pre-coded into the brain, but our thoughts are much different. We as the human race have the ability for <u>abstract thought</u>! We alone on the planet have a self awareness of whom, and what we are; we know that we are people in the human race! House pets like: dogs, cats, and even monkeys don't know who, and or what they are; even though some people say these animals do have awareness of it all. We may be able to teach our dog a new trick, but we can not teach the dog how to think <u>conceptually</u> about "<u>life</u>", we alone have these <u>thoughts</u>.

The human thought factory is running all the time on three different levels which are, in my opinion, as follows; number one is the <u>Conscious</u> part of the mind when we are awake, second is the <u>Sub-conscious</u> when we are sleeping or daydreaming, and thirdly is the electrical impulses running everything, that I'll call the "<u>Spark</u> of <u>Life</u>". We need the Spark of Life to jump start the Concious, and the Sub-conscious mind, all three form a <u>trilogy</u> that is necessary for our human thought procces. Once again man stands alone on the Earth as the "creature of thoughts!"

Do monkeys, cats, dogs or even dolphins have the abilities to think at three different levels, as we do? Well I would have to answer no, … because they haven't taken over the planet yet;.. or then again Washington D.C. is a zoo, isn't it?

The human brain is a massive network of information, where the "trilogy of thoughts" meet in our minds, to form our world view. Our world view is where all three levels of the mind are working as a whole. Most people don't even realize that their world view is what they think about most of the time. If a person thinks that he or she can do something good, and have a positive outlook, and especially a sense of humor they have a world view that is "bright, happy, and content" in who they are, and they do not need fame, or fortune to get there! If a person thinks that the world is a sad and lonely place, then their "thoughts will be sad, dark, and negative", and fame and fortune can't cure it.

Then there are those who think about fantasys all the time, never realizing they have lost touch with reality. These world views are some of the thoughts in the mind of man, one is easy to come by today; while one is hard to find! With all the negative things happening on the earth, like the wars, rumors of terrorism, and all the make-believe of Hollywood permiating every society, it is easy for people to take a negative, fantasy filled view of the world.

With thoughts like these everywhere in 2007, is that why so many people are on anti-depressants, and there are so many new fantasys for people to live out. Some of which are; body trans-mutation, where people change themselves into animals through surgery. This gives a whole new meaning to "Bat-Man" and "Cat-Woman, doesn't it? The ancient form of "body-tattooing" is everywhere, and people are putting "piercing" in their bodies, from their tongues, to their nose, and in places that I would leave to your imagination!

Can we see what is happening when dark, fantasy filled thoughts run wild in the mind of man. People will take drugs to make themselves happy, or for a new personality they copy entertainers, and some people even change their bodies just to say: "Hey world look at me, I'm someone," even if that someone is now an animal. Do sad, negative, and dark fantasy thoughts in society lead to the above mentioned behaviors? Do people relieve their insecurities and negative thoughts by self-mutilation, and drugs? For the answer just look at the world in our times! Do I have anything against these people, not at all, I feel that this is their own world view and this is how they deal with it. As long as they don't hurt other people, then to each of us, we have our own thoughts. [As for me I'll keep the ink in the bottle, and the pins in the cushion; thank-you!]

As the human mind has the ability for abstract thinking, and reasoning, which leads to our own self-awareness and even if we have a bright attitude, we can still have our thoughts influenced by a sad society.

A *chet morelli* proverb says' "All so sad, then all so sorry!" ... Are we becoming a sad and sorry excuse of a society, where the dark fantasy thoughts of others are influencing the negative world we live in? Turn on the "News" or HBO for the answer and you can see for yourself...... but there is hope!

The hope lives in the thoughts of the positive thinker, men and women that are content in who they are! These individuals have an optimistic outlook on life; as one whole package deal; they are so happy that the wrappings {the way they look} doesn't matter to these people! They don't worry about what other people think about them, because these deep thinkers are thinking about others, or how the world could be a better place. People like these are less likely to take antidepressants, or have bizarre fantasys about who they are! Bright thinkers usually have a great sense of humor, and are "quick-witted", so they can make other people smile, laugh, and most of all to think!

These thoughts of the optimistic thinkers are always a light that shines in a dark world; it has always been that way, and we pray that the thoughts of optimism will always shine on; in some of us.

The thoughts in the mind of man, some light, and some dark, the positve vs. the negative, good vs. evil, and the ultimate cosmic battle: Satan against God. These are all in the thought processes in our minds. Scientists, researchers, and doctors have tried to figure out the mind for a long time, and in many areas they have done a wonderful job, but they do not understand the reason behind the three underlining thoughts that mankind has always had; ... which are: Good vs. Evil, the positive vs. the negative, and the question of "Is there a GOD", and if so, then is there a battle going on for our souls? These questions can only be answered by each of us, in the "abstract" regions of the mind, where living cells ignite the "Spark of life"; the invisible thoughts created by electricity in our brains.

Something that can not be seen or touched, all we know is that it's always there all around, and inside us: these are some of our human thoughts.

What kind of thoughts form your world view ; are they good, or bad, are you an optimist, or a pessimist, do you believe in God, or do you have no beliefs? All these thoughts are working together to make up who you are as a person; Think about it!

GOD and the After-Life ... Is there a Forever, or is there, Nothing?

Many different views about the after-life are with us today, as they have always been. Beliefs in; heaven and hell, reincarnation, soul migration, higher or lower levels of "enlightenment", to be reborn for another try; or to be "born-again" into the Kingdom of God! We speculate, and argue about what's on the other-side; strange thing is that nobody has come back from the dead to tell us what is in the after-life; Or has someone come back from the dead to tell us about the <u>next</u> <u>level</u>! The place we call the <u>after life</u>.

People all over the globe say that they have seen and had experiences with the dead; like the ghosts of "loved-ones" or that of "historical figures." Are these ghosts real? Well to the people who see them they are and to others they are all just a psychotic delusion by those who are labeled; "weirdo's" and "nut-cases."

The list of people that are said to have seen ghosts' runs from past Presidents, to some ones grandmother. Are they all "wack-jobs" as well? I don't think all these people are weirdo's, nut-cases and wack-jobs, just because they are seeing something.

My conjecture for these "entities" is that they are malevolent beings from other dimensions that impersonate the dead, and they are the same "fallen demonic angels" from the Bible. [This subject was explored in chapter one]

Nine out of ten individuals that have had contact with ghosts are scared out of their minds by these apparitions. Does this frightening activity sound like the demons of the past here to torment us; ... or are ghosts "earth-bound spirits" doomed to walk among the living, and scare the life out of us? Paranormal activities in general are very evil in nature, just as many UFO encounters are frightening, and so are the manifestations of the devil.

I think satanic forces impersonate these ghosts and even space brothers {UFO's} to play tricks on us, as forms of malicious deception on the human race. Like a form of control that is at work in the minds and hearts of people, through their fears and gullibility in spiritual matters.

[even Christians get fooled today, that's why you should read the Bible for yourself, so God can show you how not to get fooled, read in the New Testaments book of Ephesians chap. 6, verses11 to 24 in the Bible for a reference of personal protection]

The eternal destination after death, forever somewhere or just nothing? I believe that evil would say that there is nothing after death. Evil will tell a person that they should take everything in this life, because that's all there is. God tells us that there is more to life and death, that there is a heaven and a hell. Where are you going when you die? I'll leave the answer up to you! {BOO! Did you hear something?}

Is the human thought process an electrical "spirit" that migrates from one life to another, or are we some type of universal "energy" that moves on and on like the Cosmic Ever-Ready Rabbit? The "New-Age" movement and Eastern Mysticism are a belief in that of soul-migration, where a soul moves on from one plane of existence to another. They also believe in reincarnation, where a person is re-born for another try at life. In these two ways of thinking are the thoughts of "enlightenment" as the soul travels through the cycles of life and death, and then at the highest level of existence these individuals can become a god! {Oh really a person that can't control themselves in this life wants to become a god in the next world! Well good luck, they'll need it!!!}

This is the New-Age way of thinking; the one thing about "New-age" is that it's not "new," it's "Old-Age," because the thoughts originated in ancient Babylon, Eygpt, and China, thousands of years ago!

Whether it is in this "Age," or that "Age," we as people have thoughts about ; what does happen when we die? Some people believe that there is "Nothing," once around the block of life only; this is the thought of an "Atheist." Does this make them bad people, not at all, atheists can love, and feel, just like anyone else, they just believe that the "Spark of Life" goes out, when our lights go out, no last call; just death. What if they are wrong, do they yell "Time-Out?"

In the after-life will we find heaven and hell, and do GOD and Satan really exsit? To possibly answer those questions we will look at the three major faiths on the planet in 2007, which are, Judaism, Christianity, and Islam. [And these three are in the news all the time, if you want the real news on them start reading your Bible, that's where the true story line is to be found.]!

What do these three faiths have to say about GOD and the after-life?

JUDAISM:

Judaism is the oldest of the three, dating to the time of Adam and Eve, around 4000 BC, even though Moses didn't start writing until about 1400 BC. The Jewish Holy book called the Torah, which means "The Divine Law" states that there is One GOD who created the universe, with all of the Life that's in it, and GOD makes the "Rules." Some Rabbis believe that The Lord used mathematics to create the universe and us; everything in a count, everything in codes, just like our DNA! This is why there are highly educated researchers looking into all of the "Bible-codes," because there are "codes" in everything, including us.

The Jewish belief about the after-life is that God is concerned about where our souls go at death, because God loves us and wants us home in heaven, and that Satan hates our guts; thus wanting us in hell with him. As the old saying goes; "misery wants company!" The Lord also wants us to do good works, and deeds, such as; loving one another, and trying to follow the Ten Commandments by not stealing, or murdering. Deep in His own Heart the one thing that GOD wants most of all is; GOD wants us to love Him back.

These are some of the thoughts, and beliefs of the faithful Jewish believer; which are that GOD is real, and that He is The Beginning and The End; who shall come again. To this day the Jews wait for the Messiah to come, thus bringing all prophecies to fulfillment, and to restore the nation of Israel and bring the Jewish people back home.

Well guess what: in 1948 Israel became a Nation, just as it was prophesied in the Torah, the "wandering Jews" went home. Could it be that the Messiah is coming soon? The Jews are still waiting and have a feeling that He is returning soon!

THINK ABOUT THIS:

Some Jewish Rabbis say that "When the Messiah comes, He shall interpret the Torah, every letter in the Book, even the spaces in between the letters shall be decoded by Him!

We today have codes everywhere in our modern times, will a man show up that can de-code all of lifes mysteries for us? Prophecy says' yes, so we will watch and see!

CHRISTIANITY:

"Our faith in Jesus Christ has saved us", these are words that come from the hearts and minds of every faithfull Christian, who has ever lived, or is alive today.

Christianity started about 32 AD., and centers around the historical man Jesus Christ. What real Christians believe is that Jesus Christ fulfilled all Jewish prophecies of a coming Messiah which are: Jesus was born of a virgin, He spoke God's truths about heaven and hell, then Jesus was crucified, buried, and rose from death on the third day to eternal glory!

Christians believe that their faith in Jesus Christ fulfilling the scriptures was completed at the cross and by the resurrection, where Jesus conquered sin and death. With Jesus' mission on earth completed by conquering sin and death, the purpose being to reconcile a sinful man to a righteous God.

The Christians faith is centered in Jesus Christ being God in the flesh, and He alone will save their soul from sin, and hell; which is eternal separation from God the Father, who dwells in heaven.

In Christianity it is a one to one relationship with the person of, Jesus Christ, as to what your destiny is after you die. You are either with Him, or against Him, and you will either go to heaven, or hell, you pick either Jesus, or the devil. In Christianity Jesus is the way to Heaven and Satan is the road to Hell! This man from Nazareth that many people today, believe in Him to be the LORD, and that Jesus has changed the course of history; … that is a historical fact that can not be disputed. We even split history in half at the time of Jesus' birth, from BC to AD, with Jesus in the middle!

Is He, Jesus Christ about to return to earth, as the "Biblical End-Time" prophecies predict? The Bible says that He is coming back to earth for the final battle, and I believe that to be true. Lets' keep alert and keep watch in the Middle East and wait to see what happens in this ancient Holy Land! [Please read your Bible for the heavenly perspective]

THINK ABOUT THIS:

The Jews and the Christians are looking for the return of the savior in the middle-east right now, and so are the Muslims, they are all waiting for one man to lead them to peace. Is the stage being set in the Middle-East with all the chaos and war, for a world leader to show up and bring in peace to this "hot-spot" of trouble; and then this man of peace turns the planet into hell on earth? This senario is just what the Bible predicts.

The Bible speaks of the anti-Christ showing up first on the earth before Jesus returns. Could the anti-Christ be already here in hiding, just waiting for the right moment to take over the world? Beware, and watch, but most of all PRAY, because you never know do ya!

ISLAM:

The Islamic faith is the youngest of the three major faiths and was founded by the prophet Muhammad in the about 600 AD. Islam has some of the Jewish and Christian beliefs mixed in with its writings such as; Abraham, and Moses are both found in the writings of Islam, Judaism, and Christianity, there are others but the list is very small.

In Islam the God Allah is the supreme deity who has conquering of others as one method for a person to get into heaven, and if the person does not conquer in Allah's name they will most likely go to hell.

All three faiths have one God in control, but on the roads that lead to heaven or hell there is a gigantic difference between Islam, and the Judeo-Christian view.

But because the basic concept is there we know that all of the three main faiths believe, and have thoughts, about <u>heaven</u>, <u>hell</u>, <u>GOD</u>, the <u>Devil</u>, and the <u>after-life</u>.

THINK ABOUT THIS:

All of the three main faiths that help to guide many people's thoughts today have the concept of one GOD who rules heaven and fights for our souls against the evil forces of hell. Our soul can end up in one or the other when we die, the place of the After-life. What will it be like on the other side? That may all depend on what you believe on this side. A place in time here on earth that we live in on the journey we call life; this is where we make our decision about where we go when we die! To whom this may concern from me to you, "Have a safe trip, and maybe I'll meet you there, at the next level, on the Other-Side!"

If each person would look in their heart for peace in God who has said "My peace I give to you"; then the fighting would stop. Most people though don't look to God for peace; instead they kill in the name of God. The thoughts of man apart from GOD, what type of things happen at that point, and what type of heaven or hell can we create?

The War Machine, Planet Earth,... with The New World Order....

Peace, peace, peace, we look for in the Middle-East, here in the U.S.A. we watch for terrorism, and all around the globe there are wars, and rumors of wars. Just look around and you can see that everywhere in 2007 these things are occurring, right before our very eyes! The fighting and killing has gone on since time began, so the Earth could be called a "War-machine." In the history of mankind we get on average, one year of peace, for every thirteen years of war; I think that war is winning.

We have weapons of every kind, from laser-guided missiles to nuclear bombs, and hundreds of other new "exotic" weapons; this planet is ready for war. In the USA, China, and Russia alone; all combined there are enough nuclear bombs to "blow-up" the world in one half an hour, and if we add the arsinal in the Middle-East, then they can "blow us up" in 15 minutes instead! The fuse to light-up the war machine could be in the Cradle of Life where history tells us that the human race had its beginnings; this place is the Middle-East.

In The Holy Land of today's three main faiths, here once again as always we find man at his favorite pass time; namely: war! Some believe this is the start of World War 3, people of faith believe that the "End-times" are unfolding; even the scientists who make these weapons that could "blow-up" the planet are fearful of what will happen in the future. One thing is certain in 2007 most of us agree that "something" is going to happen, but what is it, and when will it happen?

Remember this: mankind has always used the weapons he makes! Will man use his new weapons and if he does; What Then?

[Think Mushroom-Clouds Everywhere!!!]

In the Middle-East today the fighting between Arabs and Jews continues on from Biblical times, the U.S.A. is there setting up democracy, or maybe stealing the oil, and land. Whatever the reason there is always a war going on in this region of the earth, and the whole world keeps watch on the "WARS" in the Middle-East. Once again I ask; "Is this the hot-spot that lights the fuse of "Armageddon?" The Bible says that it is.

There are terrorists with deadly weapons and biological agents that can kill, sub-ways blowing-up, and planes taking buildings down; all in the name of Allah, or is the New World Order behind the scene orchestrating these acts of war on humanity? The war on terror is as deadly to the mind as it is to the body, so always watch what your governments tell you, because most lies start in high places, and wars based on lies are always the most deadly.

We spend more money on war than any other country on Earth here in the U.S.A, and why, is it because the American people like war? No that's not the answer. The answer in my opinion is: the people at the top-floor are not playing with a full deck of cards, and by their behavior we can see that their deck has "51 Jokers and a Jackass."

Are the American people the "Jackass" in the deck for not "shuffling" out more questions to our leaders as to why we fight in two, or three wars at once? You decide!

World leaders have always led their people to "War" just look at history, and the times we live in for your "proof" that this is true. "Wars, wars, and rumors of wars" they are happening more frequently in our life time, and as history repeats itself,these world leaders are taking the whole planet with them to this WAR of WARS. Here on the War Machine; planet Earth.

With more than half of the worlds population coming from the three main faiths of the Holy Land in the Middle-East, the world leaders understand that the Jews, the Christians, and the Muslims are all very important players on the world stage.

In the Middle East with the mix of religion and a violent political climate, there is a "caldron of war" brewing in this region. Add to the "brew" all of the wars going on there in 2007, and there is a very good possibility this place starts the KA-BOOM that is heard around the world! Is this the spot for the beginning of the end, will mankind's final chapter in the book of time be written here?

To answer that question we look at the Holy Books of the Jews, Christians, and Muslims, and here at least all three agree that the "Last Days" are upon us in this generation, and the "caldron of war" is here ready to explode-out its "brew!" This could mean that the "End-Times" are happening today, because with all of the weapons of mass destruction that we have, and mans continued history of war, we could be closer to the "Last Days" than we might think we are, just like the "Good Book says!"

Is the New World Order calling the "shots" in these "Last Days", or is the "Ruler of Darkness," Satan himself behind the curtain of "WAR?" If you look closely you'll see there are wars everywhere today as never before, and the "weapons" to blow-up the planet in 30 minutes are in our possession right now! So with all the weapons and all of the wars; can we safely say that our home planet the Earth is a "War-Machine?" I think it is now in 2007, and always has been; sorry to say; … but that's what I say is the truth!

THINK ABOUT THIS:

Wars can be fought for many reasons, the American Revolution was fought for "freedom" which is a "Good" cause; an "Evil" cause would be the Nazis in W.W.II, as they killed millons of people, and caused Europe to be bombed into ruins, good {God}, vs. evil {Satan}, that is the reason behind wars.

Do good people fight in evil wars? Yes they do all the time, and it is not because they are dumb, they are mislead by those who are in power. The politicians, and the militaries of the world; these are the ones who conducts these wars, and we don't question them enough on this. Why don't we? Is it because, in the shadow of the towering War-Machine our view of the truth has been darkened and then turned off? As young men and women are led off, like sheep to the slaughter, to kill or be killed in wars all over the planet. As the world leaders hold "summits" and "talks" about our "global safety," when all the while the planet is a war machine of blood, and killings. All the world leaders know this and do nothing to stop it. Why don't they stop it? They don't stop it because the government needs chaos to keep control of it's people, and the best way to do this is war, like it or not it's war, war, and more: you guessed it WAR! That's why they created the "Draft" … HELLO-OOO! [In 2008 the Senate might try to reinstate this slavery tactic once again]

I am a patriotic man and I'll fight for my God, Jesus Christ, and for what is good and righteous; but damn to the evil war, for that fight belongs to the devil. Which side of the "War-Machine" do you fight-on; good or evil; you decide; or do you let someone else make the choice for you?

Here Comes the "Chip" There Goes Your $Cash$, and Your Freedoms: The Global Community or a New World Order?

Freedom is something most Americans and people in western societies have taken for granted and that has been a really ignorant thing to do; because while Americans have not only fallen asleep at the wheel, they've also crashed the Freedom Bus into the wall of indifference. Most Americans do not even know that in the last forty years the Bill of Rights and the Constitution have been dismantled by the Washington political nightmare, that we call the government. This tax and control Frankenstein monster has stolen many of our Freedoms by destroying our two most important founding documents. How did they, the powers that be, get away with it; just say "the judges, the courts, the politicians, bankers, big-business, governments, the C.I.A. and probably a C.E.O., or two, if you dig deep enough you'll find all of them in the same Hole!

"But if the blind lead the blind; will they both not fall in the same hole?" these words were spoken by Jesus Christ over 1900 years ago. Are they true today; are the blind leaders of government, with big-business and the military, leading the world into the "Hole?"

[My advice is watch your step; and watch who you're following!!! Sign Post Just Up Ahead it says: "Watch Your Step: Governmental Bottomless Pit" … don't fall for it]

The bottom line here is these groups have <u>stolen</u> many "<u>Constitutional-Rights</u> and <u>Freedoms</u>" in the last forty years, from the 1960's through 2000, and the pace is exalting in 2007; some of the reasons why, are as follows:

We have lost some freedoms in recent decades due to the facts that "Americans love entertainment" too much, thus we are busy watching "reality shows" that are all "fake anyway," or tuning into "sports," all the time, then it's "day-time" talk shows that have "bedroom" language, or how about another "Slasher" film except this time the teen-agers get to cut up the "pervert!" So with all this "mind numbing entertainment" consuming our time, Americans and most of the world do not have a clue on what the people in charge are up too. Which in my opinion is deceptive, and a way of "brain washing" through so-called entertainment, period!

The reality of it is, at this point the mass population is under the "Witches Spell" called Entertainment that is flowing from the "media keg." As the people drink more and more of the Entertainment Brew they become intoxicated with the make believe of Hollywood from watching it on the "Boob-Tube!" Hey throw in the "porno-net" and you have a pervert's paradise of evil, which seeks out any one it can for "sexual assaults" and mischief in general. <u>These perverts especially go after children for sex, now that is evil</u>. This is the entertainment in the culture today, what a horrid reality, unless you are the Frankenstein monster.

"Ah: give me a cigar and a playboy book" said the Monster; who is the monster? I'll give you a hint; … we call it the Capital!

Have Americans become so drunk on the "Witch's Brew of Entertainment" that they don't pay much attention to what the politicians and their cohorts are taking away from the people living in the U.S.A., and the rest of the world. We here in America have lost our freedoms because we have become lazy and complacent, and the saddest fact of all is that we have thrown God out of our Nation. It's that simple.

As the old *chet morelli* saying goes: "If you don't watch your cash; someone is gonna' steal your stash, … sucker!!!"

Has the government stolen your "Freedom Cash" already, and what else have they slithered off with that belongs to us?

Soon in the near future, most likely around the year 2010, or even as early as 2008, the United States is going to make it mandatory for every citizen to have a national ID card with a micro-chip in it. This card will contain all of your personal, medical, and of course your financial information. These cards can also be used to track someone by global positioning satellites [GPS].Do you want to be monitored wherever you go by the all seeing "Eye" in the sky; namely the Government? With the new technology they can also snoop into all of our personal information. Is that what we want here in America, and the rest of the world? Well if people are that "stupid" they will get what they never expected, which is loss of their "Freedoms."

Which are the foundations of <u>Life</u>, <u>Liberty</u>, and the Pursuit of <u>Happiness</u>, as unalienable <u>Rights</u>, endowed by our Creator to live <u>Free</u>, and to pursue <u>Happiness</u> in the eyes of <u>God</u>!

These words are from our Founders of Freedom, the men and women that gave it all to start America, and they did believe that the "Eyes of God" were watching them. Sad fact coming soon is the new "Eye" in the sky which will be the government, and no longer God! God or the government; who would you want watching every move that you make? When America was founded in 1776, the Eye in the sky was GOD, by 2010 it will be the Monster called the government. Once again I ask; GOD or the Monster .... Who's ... Looking at you?

THINK ABOUT THIS:

A new National ID. Card with micro-chips that contain every bit of information about us, which by the way could be made-up. With this card the government can see you anywhere, at anytime. Locating you is easy today by using the GPS system that picks up your "signal" from the micro-chip that is in the ID card; that you now have to carry by Law.

In big and small cities here in the U.S.A., and abroad, governments are putting up cameras, and micro-phones everywhere. They {the governments} say that all of the surveillance is for our "safety" from "terrorist," and "criminals;" when the real threat is hiding behind the camera lens!

It is my opinion that in the near future you will see that the "eye" from the government is looking at you! Then who will you call on when you ask it to stop? The governmenet gave you the Card with the Chip in the first place, so they will never stop watching nor' stop the stealing of your Freedoms, once you take the Card!

When the Micro-chipped ID cards are handed out will you take one, and by doing so, have you given up your <u>Rights</u> of <u>Privacy</u>? This is by the way a big part of being Free! And if they take One Freedom history teaches us that powers in government will take all of our freedoms!

Do you want to be FREE as much tomorrow, as you are in 2007, you should think about it today; because the new surveillance society of tomorrow; is already with us today. And yes you are being watched … for your money … some say that cash has wings … well the money you carry in you pockets today, will be obsolete and, "fly-away" in the near future; because all of your Cash will be on the "CARD!"

The "Cashless Society" is coming up on the world stage very shortly, and the truth is if people do not have cash, then in reality they have no true Freedoms. Now if the government can force a national ID Card on its citizens by 2010. Why couldn't they also take all money out of circulation, and put all your money on The Card? All for "our safety and convenience" of course: says the government!

That is not a true statement because; with out "real" Gold, or Silver, all of the "paper" and the "new electronic-transfer Card cash" can and will disappear! [Just like the Stock Market Crash of "1929," that caused the Great Depression in the 1930's]

Is the US. Dollar going to collapse today as it did in the 30's, and then the "Card-Money" the government gives us will be useless also for any purchasing power. At that point the Modern Depression starts and you will have no Cash, or no Freedoms.

If the government can get our Cash onto the Card because they tell us we are in a Modern Depression, we are in BIG trouble because: No Money Means No Freedoms.

That is why the Constitution states that American money should be in Gold and Silver only! [See Article 1, sec. 8 & 10, of the U.S. Constitution!]

Not many Americans own Gold and Silver; or a copy of the Constitution, and the government knows this. 90% of the money in the world is "FIAT" electronic money anyway, which means it has no Real Cash Value like Gold and Silver do. So when all of the money gets lost in cyber-space the government will just issue; by "LAW" of course, the New "Card" that will now have all your wages put into your New Government account.

Now when you use this account the government knows everything you buy, and if they don't like what you are buying, and the fact that you are purchasing, and drinking so much "Pop!" The government will have to put a stop to this, because they know it's not good for your health, and then the "spies in the sky" will cut off your "pop supply." This sounds trivial, but it is not because the government does not have the legal right to "spy" on its own citizens. This is a violation of the <u>Fourth Amendment</u> in The <u>Bill</u> of <u>Rights</u> which states this <u>Truth</u>:

"<u>The Right of the People to be Secure in their Person, houses, papers, and effects, against unreasonable searches and seizures; Shall Not Be Violated</u>'; [caps. are mine]

What this says is that "We the People" can not be "spied on by the government", it violates our Rights as American citizens and it is Illegal!

In other words the government can't spy and then take away your "pop supply", or anything else that is yours! What the government is doing now is "Unconstitutional" and so are many of the laws that they are making all over America today. According to my own survey most Americans disagree with these laws anyway! These tax collecting, and corporate "money mobsters" that make all of these laws, which are designed more for control, than for fighting criminals and terrorists, are up to no good, just look at this:

There is a new law from the Supreme Court that was passed in 2006 that says it's all right to take your private property and build anything that will generate "tax-dollars" for the government. The "Eminent Domain" Ruling means that the government can "steal" your property any time they want to and Not Compensate you for the Cash Value of your Property! This once again is Unconstitutional, these crooks and criminals are a big evil on the insides of our so-called, halls of Justice.

Take a peak at how much control these people in power have already taken from the American people, as we are Monitored from the cradle to the grave: Read On …

When we are born there is the Birth Certificate, if you get married you'll need another called the Marriage License, the first one is free, oh, the second one will cost you $125. Then we have the Death Certificate, which means for the dead guy taxes are over so they can't get his money now. That's not a problem because plan B, will get the $Cash$ for the government. The plan is this…. SURPRIZE: "The Estate Tax", which Taxes you when you are "dead"; of course! These crooks in the government take a big chunk of money anyway whether you're alive or dead, the tax-man cashes in on everything. You see these "Thugs", calling themselves politicians; are for the most part after the money, that's where the power is. So if they can get the money, sorry to say there goes the Freedoms right behind as the global community starts to emerge here in America, orchestrated by power hungry people in the control room of the War-Machine, here on planet Earth.

Will Freedom always Ring, or is the Liberty Bell being cracked beyond repair? Will the New World Order crack it in half and then the Liberty Bell will ring no more for Americas Freedoms?

Author's side-bar ...

The United States has LOST 80% of it's manufacturing business in the last 20 years, because of our so called politicians selling out the American worker to other countries; especially China. If America can not manufacture its own goods, then who will? Remember the good old "Made in the U.S.A" sticker, well that's gone now and forever, it has been replaced with "Made in" China, Mexico, Japan, ect.., but those are going away also, to be replaced by this; "Made by The New World Order!" [The government will say that this is just the "New Global Community"; will you believe these same people that took your $Cash$ and with it your Freedom. A time will come when you have to give your "finger-print" just to buy bread and milk; who's the "prisoner" at this point in time?]

No Jobs, no cash, no Cash, no freedoms, no Freedoms, and then; you are a "prisoner!"

The Wars We Never Win ... So Why Fight Them?

"Wars, and rumors of war, Nation against nation; Brother against brother; famines, diseases, and Natural disasters" this saying from the Bible is in reality what is happening in 2007. Natural disasters [acts of God] are out of our control. What about others? Can we control Brother, against, brother, Nation vs. nation, or the Wars and rumors of them?

In Western societies; especially the United States, we do try to control the other Nations as world policemen, thinking that the whole world should be like us. We are a Nation vs. nations in wars that are going on right know, so the USA is trying to control world democracy. What about Brother vs., brother these are Social Problems; but we call them Wars. Such as: "the War on Drugs" or the "War on Poverty"; with more Wars on "Racism" and "Illiteracy". These are not Wars they are Social Problems; they are a "Scourge" that inflicts pain, and devastates a country.

In a war there is an enemy, in social problems, we have problems, not enemies. These modern social problems are turned by politicians into "tax money vacuum cleaners" that suck-up the Tax money. Then the politicians tell the American people that they spend it on all of the WARS. We are told that so we will have to keep-on "fighting" the battles, but not with solutions from the name calling professionals, namely most politicians, no their solution is that we here in America have to pay the cost with higher taxes. The problem is the government has never won any of the Wars yet! Never the less the government fights these "losing" battles on and on; with tax money that is destroying the United States Middle Class! That doesn't matter to the government; they can lose all the Wars and still win; because we are so DUMB that we keep paying them with our taxes.

[Federal taxes are illegal; there is no Law on the books anywhere, to make you pay taxes on your labors with a Federal tax. The tax is only for Big-Business.... The FEDS Income Tax is Illegal and is Unconstitutional; because the 16th amendment was not ratified by two-thirds of the States, which are needed to change the Constitution ... If you don't believe me call the IRS and ask them to tell you the Law that states that you have to pay Federal Income Tax, they will never give you the Law; because there is NO LAW! YOU DO NOT HAVE TO PAY FEDERAL INCOME TAX! ... The system is all VOLUNTARY! ... see page 3 of the 1992 forms and 1040 Instruction book issued by Internal Revenue Service, the Commissioner of the I.R.S. states, paragraph 2, sentence 1: "You are among the millions of Americans who comply with the Tax Law VOLUNTAR-ILY". Also see IRS tax code 26 chap.1 the 4-01-2003 edition].

Why is it with all of the trillions of dollars that the government says it spends on these wars, then taxes the American worker more, and more to fight these wars, then the government still loses every war it fights; anyway? I say why fight wars that are never won. If the wars are not being won, where is the Illegal Tax Money going? The "dirty money" is going into the "vacuum cleaner-bags" for most politicians; with others; which are their pockets, and their bank accounts: that is my opinion! As the politicians funnel the money from taxes to themselves, and make all the laws that make it "legal" for them to have access to the real Gold and Silver. This Gold and Silver belongs to "We the People", keep that in your mind when you file your taxes.

Question, have you ever seen a poor politician in Washington DC, think about it: OK times up, ... I haven't either ... truth is: there aren't any ...! Don't believe me. Just take a look at your local ones, how poor are they?

THINK ABOUT THIS:

The plaque at the Statue of Liberty reads something like this: "Give Me the poor, which want a better life and the castaways, so that they may have a home; and give Me all of the slaves; who long to be free".

The Pilgrams, the Immigrants, and the Slaves were poor; and they were all cast away from the world, then settled here, in America; so we should "Thank God" for these Freedom Pioneers, who let freedom ring for us today; but they warned us to not to let the government, big-business, and the military become one. This is called a <u>Military Industrial Complex</u> {M.I.C.} that will grow out of greed and power to take all of our Silver and Gold.… Have they done this already?

OH, No! I have to go check my "piggy bank" The Wolf in sheeps clothing is here with his hammer! OH, No, I'm too late my Gold, and Silver are gone, but the Wolf left his "Calling-Card".…

Let's read what's on the Card; it says: "The Wolf" fights Wars; which include: "Crime, Drugs, Poverty, Racism, Illiteracy; and of course Terrorism." Fighting these wars cost money, that's where you, the American People came in to mind; thanks for the Silver, and Gold, sorry about the "piggy-bank" gotta run.… # @!"

.… the Wolf is always running to Wars that it never wins.… and the ones with the "piggy-banks" pay for them! Smart as a Fox; no: Wise as "The Wolf" … and you better "Pray" that you are not the "night-stalker's" next "Prey" … Oh, you pay taxes too; then you, and I, are already victims of the Wolf … [And his nick-name is IRS or M.I.C.]

Walk Don't Run …; Are We Moving too Fast?

Sociology 101: Circa; The Present.
Place: Any modern city, or suburb
Reason: How fast can we go?

In just 100 short years we have gone from "horse-power" at about 30 miles per hour, too, "high speed air-travel" at 300 mph, and more; now that's Fast. This is not fast enough for mankind because the Space-Shuttle orbits the Earth at 17,000 miles per hour, but we shall stay here on Earth, to see, how "Fast" our modern society is moving!

The Fast-lane is used in traffic, the inter-net is a "High-speed" information highway, stores, gas-stations, and restaurants, are all open 24/7, to keep our "FAST-PACED" society moving at an all time historical pace, that has never been done before! Do we think we are "Super-man", that we can move so Fast as to Fly? Well we could end up moving so quickly that we trip over our own "two feet", and then we will not be leaping over "tall buildings in a single bound", instead we'll be falling flat on our "faces."

Fast-Food joints are everywhere, and why is this? When the service in these joints isn't FAST, it's just so Sl-l-o-ow: [that's an oxymoron you moron … nyuk

... nyuk ... nyuk ... Ah; lighten up life is too short to be humorless, so at times I am a stooge!]!

Fast, faster, fastest, the pace always quickens; it is almost as if we can't slow down, as we run on in the "Age of Speed!" We rush to get to work then we rush to get home: that's way they call it "The Rush hour"; say Duh now! We rush to this "appointment," and to that "event" with reckless abandonment, that we behavior like "naughty children" who are on a "sugar high." With rude behaviour on the rise in society we can easily see that all this "rushing around" has led to things like: "Road-rage", anger management programs, pills being popped by children with A.D.D., to the Pharmasist that gets hooked on his own pills! Now that doesn't ADD up! Whatever the case may be, everyone is taking drugs it would seem from all the drug commercials on cable TV. Oh but that's O.K. is the word from the Food and Drug Administration, even though the side-effects with most of these drugs can sometimes be fatal!

With 1 out of 3 people on some kind of drug, it is as if everyone in our society is rushing to and fro like a ping-pong ball flying in a hurricane. We know where the ball started before the hurricane struck, we just don't know where the ball will end up after this storm.

The hurricane force use of drugs in the world today is getting out of control; whether they are prescription or others; there are drugs everywhere. That's why there are Drug Stores, and "dealers" on almost every other corner. We in society are so use to the drugs that we are lulled to sleep in the "EYE" of the hurricane, that we forget there is another side to the storm of drug use!

The "Drug induced Age of speed," and faster, and faster and faster we go, just like the spinning of the hurricane. We could be in the Eye of the hurricane right now with the other side of the storm about to hit us, as society is drugged into a dependence stupor from all of these drugs. Then before we know it the society is just a bunch of trance like "zombies" running around. Oh we already have "mall-zombies" don't we! "Mall-Zombies" in our society rushing around; hey just think one could even be an "air-traffic controller" ... think about it. Oh you can't ... Because you have to "rush-off!" Oh so sorry you had to leave so fast ... on a Jet-Plane you say! But who's watching the Radar ...?

In the Studies that take years to complete, and millions of dollars, the modern medical, sociological, and scientific researchers are telling us that we should "Slow-Down" for our Health, and we should stop the "Fast-Pace" and Enjoy Life; GEE ; I could have told us that for Nothing! Now lets' all say: "Common Sense," at No Cents Cost!

As for a relaxing moment even doctors will tell you to have a beer or two, maybe a glass of wine, or even a stiff drink. Just don't go over board and become a drunk! Also keep in mind that these same doctors could make you a Prozac person!

THINK ABOUT THIS:

Does all this "Speed" give us happiness? Even if it does we use it fast anyways in this age of instant gratification! We speed up the clock by "rushing" all over the place in high gear, then we <u>Complain</u> that we <u>Have No Time</u>; is everyone "NUTS" ... or is this the by-product of our "fast-paced" society?

With all of the technologies that we have, and at the pace we are running as the human race, will we finish the race behind our own technologies? Have we been given too much, too soon, and at the speed we are going will we run right passed the finish line, and never even realize that we've won? As we become consumed by the fast pace of modern life, will we out-run ourselves; or will we tire-out even before we ever get to the end of the race?

In Aseops' fable the slower Tortoise beats the faster Rabbit in their race through the forest.

The Tortoise who looked around and really enjoyed the forest had a good time getting to the finish line, plus the Tortoise won the race ...

As for the Rabbit he had a terrible time, because he was in a hurry to win, and he did not even see the forest ... and the Rabbit lost the race anyways ...

In the Forest of Life who are you, the Tortoise or the Rabbit? Before you answer ... Oh Look what I found a "riddle" that I have also, just made-up!

Here is the *chet morelli* Riddle:

"You are awaken to a terrible hunger by a digital cell-phone that won't stop ringing; first you turn off the phone; then rush to feed your hunger; and you end up at a place where the first words you hear are: "CAN I TAKE YOUR ORDER" ; you then get the Fast-Food, and Speed off to work; ;speed, speed,speed, but you never have enough time ... who are you ... well you're definitely not a Tortoise!.... So how does the Tortoise get his order then? Well He orders at home in the "Shell" and he's ordering Rabbit stew, why? The Rabbit lost, and was "stewing" of course!!! ... END OF RIDDLE ... and now the Moral of the riddle ...!

Do you want to run around crazy for the finish line in life that may be a dead-end; or would you rather want to slow-down and sit back in your Easy-chair, then be thankful that you are in the race of life to start with. Do you enjoy your forest of life, or are you moving around the forest so fast that it is being cut-down all around you and you can't even see it? Do you know what's being cut-down?

It's the trees of life's experiences that are being cut out of the lives of people that are always in a hurry; in this "Age of Speed."

If you slow down to enjoy the trees you will have memories of each tree.If you keep a fast pace in the forest the trees will be gone before you ever really looked at them.... END OF MORAL ...

Are you a Tortoise or a Rabbit ... because it's your life and the trees are your "Human Experiences" that you are living out every moment; so try to enjoy them! Are you moving to fast, or are you moving at a slow pace? Either way; I hope you enjoy your "Forest of Life." I would recommend to SLOW DOWN and make Memories of the Heart; those are the Trees in the Forest my friend!

Tic,Tic,Tic ... The Clock Moves On ...

Here we are at One minute to midnight on the Present clock, only a Tic away from the Future. Where do the hands of time move to now, where will the sands of time fall? Is the Earth, our home, on a collision course with the prophecies that are in the Bible, are the "Last Days" upon us? Is this the beginning of World War III? With wars on the increase, and China together with Russia conducting war games, aimed at a "first-strike" against the United States, World War III might be on the near horizon. That's one thing the C.I.A. knows is true and does nothing about.

What does the C.I.A. stand for? It stands for "Controllers in Action"; and this is what they have to say, and what they do.

"Hey look; nothing up my sleeve.... PRESTO ... AMERICO ... LOOK-O ... We have your Private Info ...!"

They can "watch" and "monitor" the American Citizen all the time with all the new high-tech. surveillance system's installed everywhere, the "Eye" of big government is looking at everyone now. Cameras in places we don't even see, are watching everything all the time. With that said; then our own government has the nerve to tell us: "they {the government} did not have enough intelligence about Sept. 11th 2001 to stop the Twin Towers from being hit." They can spy on Americans with precision accuracy, but all the high-tech surveillance and so-called intelligence by the C.I.A. didn't work that day, in September of 2001, to stop the terrorism. This doesn't make sense to me! Do you see an "illusion" being formed here? I do. The "illusion" is: they {governments} spy and lie, and Americans die. Sad fact is, this is for real, think about it!

Will our leaders of today do what most have done in the past, throw a party while the whole world spirals out of control with biological, chemical, and nuclear weapons? They wouldn't throw a party while we all get killed! They wouldn't be that "heart-less" would they? When we elect our leaders into office to protect our <u>Constitutional Rights</u>, which are: to <u>Pursue Life</u>, <u>Liberty</u>, and <u>Happiness</u>, and we can't have any of these if we are dead! So the politicians wouldn't let us die and throw a party would they?

Answer is, just watch the "Parties" that the American politicians throw now! [These groups even take on the title of a different "Party"]

OH; LOOK WHAT I FOUND, A LIST OF SOME PARTIES: Let's read it:

The Democratic Party and the Republican Party, both have Conventions{ Parties?} that cost about 10 million dollars or more, this is not a "convention", it's a CON-GAME. The list continues: Dinner Fund Raisers that cost into the thousands of dollars per person, a party here and a dinner there and all with big-bucks, for the "Fat-Cats" in politics. They eat like kings and queens. Yet right here in the U.S.A. we fight a war on "poverty!" Sound like a Con-Game or what? I think the "educated masters" that perform the slight of hand magic tricks; are fiddling at the "parties" as the world burns with war!

Like it or not the "party" goes on in every Capital city and in all the political circles here in the U.S.A., you see we pay, and they play! As these "magicians" play the tricks of deception on the world stage, they are the ones that manipulate people's "world views" for them. With governmental propaganda, and lies, as the managed media helps to propogate this agenda which is in my view: governmental control! [Unconstitutional think about it!]

Here are some examples of this "trick" us, and "treat" themselves to a life style of the Rich and the Famous. That's why they are always taking the so called "Photo-Ops," as to show us the great job they are doing for THE PEOPLE! If you believe their story that they are for us; then I have some Fools Gold to sell you from; "Fort. NOTS."

In the war on racism that seems to be going on all the time according to the government, we the American people are the so-called "Racists" and that's the furthest thing from the truth as they can get us! Truth is most of us Americans are not "racists," Period! I am a fifty year old "American man" who has "friends of every age and color." Now that's a "Rainbow Coalition", and most other Americans feel this way also! What color am I? Color blind of course, because that's the only way to see all of the colors in the "Rainbow of People" and that's what makes Americans great people!

The government and the News Media would have us think otherwise, as they continually tell us about "racism" and play over and over again, a million times the same story. Which is that we are all "racists", the onslaut of this "brain-washing "goes on everyday, think about it! The bigger the Lie, and the More often that it's Told, then the more likely people are to Believe the Lie!

Is there "Racism" in America? Yes there is, but NOT as much as the "magicians" in government and the media would like us to believe.

Over 1900 years ago Jesus Christ said this "A House Divided will soon Fall", the Master of one-line strategy has "warned us" about this in house [country], fighting, [racism?]. Do the powers that be divide us for their own gain by yelling RACISM all the time? I truly believe that this is exactly what they do!

Chaos, [the house is falling], leads to control, [oh we the government can help], which leads to absolute Power to the "helpers." Governments start the chaos, and end up with the control. Do you see a "Mind-Freak" illusionist scheme unfolding? First you see Chaos; move the Curtain and now you see Control, all an Illusion? Maybe not, but if it turns out to be true don't call me a "freak" cause I warned you!

Have we become so far removed from the truth that the "eerie atmosphere" of our modern age is from all the lies being told? Are we living in a reality that is being "made-up" for us by the "Author of Lies" ... Satan! That my friend you can decide; because it's your "world-view" that's at stake, and your Eternal Destiny may be involved!

Governments, tell us what we can and can not do such as: "buckle-up" for you're "Safety," then they allow cars that go 120 miles per hour onto the roads, and inform us that everything is "safe" because; they have tested the safety-factor on "Crash-Dummies". The fact of the matter is, in many of the tests done on high speed vehicle crashes, the end results are deadly. Even with the "seat-belts." on the "crash dummies." Who's the real dummy here? I'll give you a hint; you and I are sitting with Him, or Her, right now! Now that makes me nervous can I have a smoke? WHAT ARE YOU NUTS THAT'S AGAINST THE LAW: NO SMOKING! THE GOVERNMENT SAYS SO, REMEMBER THAT:

Let me ask you a question: "Do you really think that the lowest IQ's in the history of America, which are happening in our generation, are an accident?" Guess again, this is all by Government design; dummy!

The man who brought about our "Public education" system name was Dewey, and he was an atheist who hated Christianity. He was a promoter of "racsim, socialism, and a one-world government". Most Americans do not know about Deweys beliefs, because the "Magicians" [public education] keep their "tricks" [political correctness] a secret! The question is do-we follow Dewey? [I think we already have become a nation of Duh-we's]

So the next time you see a yellow school bus, filled with children, off to a so called; "good public education", in a system founded by an individual who was anti-Christian, and he was a racist. This man Dewey also firmly believed in a one world government, all very un-American. Is this the environment that we should allow the children to be taught in?

IN GOD WE TRUST is one of the U.S.A.'s mottos and I believe in this statement. The question is: will this motto last? If children are taught in an atheistic system that is: Anti-GOD, and Anti-American, where will that lead America and the free world? To answer that I would ask you to <u>Think About This</u>:

On the "yellow buses" in America rolls the Future, and what new world will they encounter, or create with the education they are receiving today? ... Well speaking of the Future ... ours is coming soon! As for The Present ... CLOCK # TWO ... Tic ... Tic ... Tic ... Has Now ... Stopped ...

Chapter Three

Clock Three: The Future
Where Do We Think We Are
Going?

The Past Is Now History: Welcome to the Future ...

Where has the human race run to now? Has man reached the stars before his home planet the Earth has melted-down from the sun, or has mankind been destroyed by nuclear weapons? Has man found a way to live in peace, or did man escape from war to other dimensions? Did the technology of the past come back to haunt the future, has God saved man from himself, or did man give himself over to Satan? As we step into the Future will we find Paradise, or Hell on Earth?

Well to find out the answers to this entire question we must first take a walk on the Earth of the Future; now known as "THE PLANET OF THE PLUG-IN'S:"

Introduction to: "The Planet of the Plug-Ins".... "2111 A.D."

The year is now 2111 AD the human race had started the 22nd century with the final phase completed of "Computer/Brain Technology," [C/b tech.], which is a medical procedure that completely merged the mind of man with that of a computer; or aptly named "artificial human intelligence."

From the 1960's through 2110, in the 150 years of computer development, combined with the last 50 years of brain research surgery, man has merged his mind to the computer. To the ultimate point of becoming a god! [Or so they thought]

In the year 2097 a break-through in[C/b tech.],was made by code #0017, [all names were out-lawed in 2075 by the World Code Council. No names, just Codes]. The new technology discovered by, reshercher code # 0017, who pioneered this frontier with C/b tech., had once again treaded the uncharted regions of man and machine with the development of Nano-Light Transfer, [N/L-T].

This new technology [N/L-T] allowed mankind to transfer neurons, [the neuro-transmitters], of the brain directly into the "Master Computer Code" [MCC] called "Codex InfinaNet" [C.I.N]! This meant that all of the information contained in the Codex InfinaNet could be transferred to the human brain through generated Nano-Light in the computer. This system all worked in conjuction with the electricity already present in the brain! The Codex InfinaNet was the data-base that held all of mans knowledge, emotions, and activities of the past. This information was all stored in the Master Computer Code, [MCC].

With the discovery of the Nano-Light Transfer, [N/L-T] man could access everything that man has done, thought, and felt before. Everything imaginable to man could be attained, why man could even become God! With the N/L-T man was now inside the C.I.N.. walking around in his own mind; realizing the thoughts from so long, long ago, that "We can become gods", and now this was all just in mankind's reach; ... or so he thought!

The Codex InfinaNet, [C.I.N.], was the heart-beat of the Earth with hook-up terminals everywhere for people to plug-into. This was done so they could access needed information for the daily work activities. They could also have every pleasure imaginable for a person to experience, and all this would happen when you; "plugged-in!"

Everything and anything was in the C.I.N. data-base, the complete history of the human race, and all this information was now transferable to the human brain. Every book, movie, CD Rom, soft-ware program, historical events were all in holographic images. The music, the art's, the full spectrum of human activities since The Dawn of Civilization, all of this information could be transferred to the mind of the Plug-Ins!

The C/b tech. was old technology and anyone could access it. But the new teck, N/L-T., was only for the "Chosen-ones!"

During the plug-in phase to the NEW Nano-Light Transfer Unit, a person could experience "out of body" travel that would allow the user to transverse "space-time" ... which up to this point man had never done. Men and Women could now literally "walk" to the moon in a "digital simulation" a holographic person in the electrical impulses of the Universe itself! This is called The Nano-Light Transfer Zone.

As the N/L-T. Unit was working in concert with the Codex-InfinNet [C.I.N.], mankind was creating a new race of people; called "Codex Humanus!"

Codex Humanus are only those few "Chosen-ones", who were on the World Law Council, and The Specialists, which numbered about 1000 in 2102, but by the year 2108 the number had dropped to 20! The reason for the drop in members was due to the new Law by the World Law Council, in 2108, which stated:"Only the highest Code numbers on the Council and or a Specialist could have access to the Nano-Light Transfer. This is the new Law and everyone has to obey, except the chosen few! [LAW CODE: C.I.N. #1 ...]

The Council members and Specialist, were now also called "THE CODES", this was their way of informing the people that they alone were the Masters of the Codes, and only the "Chosen-ones" could enter the Nano-Light Transfer Zone![N/L-T./Z.]

This new Law also meant that only 20 Council members and Specialists could use the new technology. That left out 980 council members and their families who were now unable to use the Transfer Zone. End result was that these 980 were now similar to the 2 million or so people left on Earth in 2102; and these "people" were a "mind-controlled" Human Resource group called the Plug-Ins. Now by the Law all of these people could only access information that the Council members had the Specialists "code" into the Master Computer Code of [C.I.N.]. The Council could Code-In whatever they wanted the the "Plug-ins" to think and to do!

If anyone was caught breaking the LAW then they would have to "un-plug" themselves permanently from the Codex InfinaNet. This was a death sentence of the Mind, Body, and Spirit, as one would then have to wander around aimlessly as a "un-plugged"; which was the lowest level of society.

With 20 Council Members making the LAWS, with the medical and scientific "Specialists," basically running the known World of only 144,020 people in the year 2111; amazingly everything seem to be working smoothly with this small population on the planet. Reason was; the elimination of war in 2024, that allowed the human race to survive!

Mankind conquering war, 144,020 people living in peace and harmony in a Shan-gri-la Land of computer controlled happiness; as it was said by the plug-ins: "Heaven is here on the earth, under the dome!" The plug-ins were very content with their lives, as there were only 2 known cases of people beinging un-plugged in the 60 years of the plug-In program. The "plug-ins" have a mantra which is: "To plug-in is to live; to un-plug is to die!"

No wars, no plagues, no famines, which added up too, happy people all living in peace, and happiness here on the earth. Nice ride and smooth sailing, until those with the "Codes"; namely the Council Members and the Specialists wanted much more than peace and happiness. So they went looking for it and then, wandered to deep into the "Nano-Light Transfer-" in their attempt too become God!

What happened when man attempted to become God? Did he succeed or fail? To answer we will start in the year 2024, and end in 2111, on The Planet of the "Plug-Ins."

YEAR: 2024 …

It all began just like the conspiracy group of scientists had predicted in 2005. What they had predicted would happen, did happen. Which was massive "brain damage" from the use of "cell-phones," … but it went much deeper than that. It became the plague that devastated the Earth from 2020, through 2024, that killed or permanently damaged the brain and the DNA of 9/10th of the world's population. The results were that just fewer than 10 million people were left on the planet!

<u>Mass In Neuro Density That Is Killing</u>, the "MIND TIK," was the name given to the plague, because of what it did to its victim's. The Mind Tik caused a breakdown in brain tissue which led to massive tumors, and also caused DNA structure mutation from the "micro-waves" emitted by cell-phones. This caused a LOUD TICKING SOUND IN THE PERSONS HEAD, like this … TIC … TIC … TIC … all the time … which would drive the individual crazy. Many committed suicide, and others were drugged until death took over! This was the worst plague in the history of mankind, with over 5 billion people dying, and that's not the end of it because; the MIND TIK was passed on to children through tainted DNA from their parents.

The worldwide ban on cell-phones in 2022 stopped the cause of the plague; but its human devastation and effects would linger on well after the problem was gone. After the ban on cell phones every person on earth needed to be "chipped" with a new micro-chip that could be used to communicate with; just like a cell-phone. The Phone-Chip was discovered in 2023 at the Institute for Mind Research in, Rochester, N.Y., and most people were implanted with the phone-chip by years' end in 2024.

By 2024 the world was just starting to realize the daunting task to rebuild the Earth was all in the hands and minds of those few who were left! Everything was in chaos and the people left on the earth knew they had to cooperate with each other or the human race was nearing the finish line. Meaning if they didn't cooperate with eachother then the human race would be over, and over very soon!

In December of 2024 the United Nations was abolished, and a new organization was created by a delegation of representatives from all corners of the globe; it was named The World Council. The Council had 1000 representatives from every walk of life; such as the nurse, the author, the pizza guy and the day care lady. All of the people that make up our everyday lives, were now in charge of the World! These people believed they could do a better job than the governments that fell along with the billions of people, during the Mind-Tik plague.

The first order [law] passed by the World Council on December 31st of 2024 was to "Abolish all wars and use the nuclear weapons for energy needs of the new world." [Law # 1: 12/31/2024]This was the first new law of a brand new world, and there would be other laws to come.

YEAR: 2050 …

The Earths population has stabilized at about 7 million people in 2035, from the 10 million 10 years ago. Everyone on the planet now lives in, and around three major cities. Main reason was their "prime global" locations, and the fact that these Cities were in close proximity to each other. This was all a perfect location to accommodate the small population that was left on the earth. These three cities have agricultural resources in the surrounding country sides for farming; they also have modern medical and scientific facilities that are already in place. This whole location also has an excellent road system for quick and easy travel. The reason they needed a good highway system was that: all air travel was "outlawed" in 2035. This is when the Three New Cities of the world were inhabited with the 7 million people left on the Earth, while the rest of the planet went back to being just "wild", no people only animals and nature. No more L.A., New York, Paris or London, all of them were uninhabited "wild" places!

These three cities which are the known World in 2035 are: Pittsburgh, PA, Rochester, NY, and Niagara Falls, US and CAN. The World Council picked these cities and put it into Law #101, 9/11/2030; also in the Law were the reasons why they chose these three cities.

Pittsburgh was chosen for the city of manufacturing and textiles, Rochester was picked because it has the medical, scientific, and technological research facilities that are already in place, and both of these areas have excellent farmland that surrounds them. The city of Niagara Falls would be the city of The World Law Council, and the Cultural/Entertainment Center of the World. All three Cities were close with car travel, within 8 to 10 hours of each other. These cities were all by water, the Great Lakes for unlimited fresh water, and with the mighty Niagra River plunging over The Falls generating all the Hydro-Electric Power that is needed to run all three of these cities. Just as these Cities did before the plague hit, they were up and running, as the lights, and power were staying on in this brave new world.

Putting the Law# 101 into effect was immediate as the re-organization project began in October 2030. The project was completed by 2034, and all of the people that were left on the earth had to fly into one of the New Cities by December 31st of 2034. Due to the fact that after that date all "Air-Travel is Outlawed {by the Law, of course}," and if you didn't make the dead line then you were stuck in the "wild" to fend for yourself.

When people arrived they were assigned a city depending on their individual skills, or lack there of! If you were a scientist, doctor or a reasercher, you would go to Rochester, a tool and die maker, or a shoe manufacturer would end up in Pittsburgh. Farmers of produce, dairy and livestock would live, and work in the areas around the cities. With Niagara Falls being designated as "The Get Away City for Enjoyments," and the "Seat of the World Law Council."

By the year 2045 the New Three City World was up and running like a "fine tuned" time piece. In the 20 years since the Mind-Tik plague almost wiped out the human race, mankind had done the impossible; they survived, and were living in peace. As time went on there was a problem going on though with children born during the Mind-Tik plague. This problem had the Council, and the Specialists very concerned!

In the year 2050 it seemed very clear to the researchers in Rochester that the children born during the plague years had a genetic mutation in their DNA that made their IQ's that of a 12 year old. The problem for the researchers was that these were young men and women that were in their 20's, and they should have higher IQ's by this age! The researchers were also concerned that this group would pass on the DNA mutation to other generations. The main problem now was the sheer number of people in this age group that have low IQ; s; was about 2 million young adults, almost 1/3 of the population. What could the research Specialists do, as most of these people with the lowest IQ's were getting more and more uncooperative in society? This was unacceptable behavior by Law, as The Council demanded complete obedience by the population. The Council needed a solution and they put the top Specialists to work on the problem.

In October of the year 2050 Dr. Crazsine and his team of Specialists at the Rochester Institue of Mind Research, working night and day finally perfected a procedure called: Computer/brain Technology. [C/b tech.]

Computer/brain Technology [C/b tech.] was a procedure to raise a persons IQ to at least 90, and this was greatly needed at this time, because the uncooperative ones were getting worse! The C/b tech. procedure was to surgically attach a micro-chipped circuit board to the person's brain through the base of the skull. This would leave an in-put plug exposed outside of the skin that allowed a person to be plugged into a pocket sized computer. The computer could be programmed differently for each personality and it was all perfectly "safe;" ... according to the Specialists.

The surgeries started in late November of 2050, just as a major blizzard slammed into the Rochester area. As the storm roared outside, the first recipients of the of the C/b tech. circuit board implants were on the operating table. They were four men in their 20's with IQ's of 70 or less. These were the first "Plug-Ins!" The surgeries were a success and the implants worked so well that Dr. Crazsine and his team continued with the surgeries well into the next two decades.

Mankind and his computer were starting to merge into one mind in 2050, even though some of the Specialists at the time questioned the ethics of it. That didn't matter because they were informed by the Council that they had to do it. The reason being is that all the residual brain damage in young people from the plague is "Dumbing-Down" the society, and by Not doing the C/b tech. procedures it would jeopardize the future. Why it could ruin everything that the human Race has stood for; namely "survival." The Council stepped in ultimately with a LAW passed on November 30th 2050, which made the implants mandatory for any one with a low IQ. Law # 10222 11/30/2050 was now on the books.

YEAR: 2060

By the year 2060 the Plug-Ins were doing all of the manual work in the "Triple Cities" as the only inhabited places on Planet Earth were now called! As a new generation was being born to parents who were already plug-ins, this meant that their children would also have to be implanted at the age of, 3 years old.

Dr. Crazsine and his team perfected "infant circuit boards" {icb's} in January of 2059. On March 21st 2059 the Council passed a Law that made it mandatory for all children at the age of 3 to become a "plug-in." The previous age by Law of plugging-in was 12 years old. The New LAW # 203010 3/21/2059 was obeyed by everyone.

Inside the rooms of the Council and in the corridors of The Rochester Institute of Mind Research the Plug-ins were known as BOBS, which was short for, "circuit Board On the Brain". The members of the Council and the Specialists were becoming more, and more arrogant as time marched on in the new world of the plug-ins.

By the end of 2060 the new central data-base was up and running, sending out orders and information to all of the plug-ins. This data-base was called the Master Computer Code or MCC! With the new data-base in operation all of the plug-ins were able to work much better, as the codes they were receiving were more detailed than ever before. They were also much happier because of the new "pleasures" that they could experience when they plugged-into the X-Plug Terminal; ... where lasciviousness was the norm. The plug-ins were programmed by the C.I.N. Computer to plug into Terminal X, because it was for pleasurable "Sex." This kept the plug-ins happy and working for the system, also the Council knew it created more "plug-ins" to keep the system running.

YEAR: 2065

2065 was labeled the "Year of the DOME" by the Council, as the mammoth building project was now complete, with all of the labor being done by the plug-ins. The work was completed by July of 2065 as the whole downtown district in Niagara Falls had been enclosed with a network of small domes. All of the interior and exterior was of a gold metallic color. The domes were also pyramidal in shape and resembled a bees "honeycomb." Inside the dome it seemed like the plug-ins were the worker bees doing everything in a "buzzing" atmosphere of control. With the Specialists and the Council members acting as the Queens, and the Kings in this world of the plug-in worker bees. These few really enjoyed having all of the power in the world now, as they were in complete control; ... or so they thought!

YEAR: 2070 ...

The Earths population is dropping by the year 2070, as there are only 4 million people left, and 99% of them are plug-ins; half person, half computer. With the New Master Computer Code {MCC} and The Codex InfinaNet {CIN} Data-Base, the plug-ins could do more complicated things: such as brain surgeries on other plug-ins. The codes were becoming more complicated as Dr. Crazsine and his teams were perfecting the Codex InfinaNet data-base which held the information that was needed for coding into the plug-ins. Which included anything from cooking gourmet meals for the Kings and Queens to performing complicated surgeries on other plug-ins. The C.I.N. Codes were giving more and more meaning to life as they allowed the Specialists and the Council to program more and more information into the plug-ins, and be able to monitor them like a "Living Experiment."

The Council and the Specialists live like Kings and Queens watching the plug-ins do just about everything, except "think" on their own. In this bizarre reality that earth had become; nobody could see what was happening, because everyone was happy. No wars or fighting, everyone was taken care of, and all was normal as time marched on. As time was moving forward the codes inside the computer were becoming more complicated, and that kept the Council and the Specialists in charge of everything with total control over society!

In the year 2075 another new Law was passed by the Council on September 30th 2075 that stated: "From this point in time and forward all Names are Outlawed, all Council Members and Specialists shall have CODE NUMBERS instead of names; and all plug-ins shall be known as BOBS [circuit Boards On the Brain] in a sequence of random numbers. All of the numbers were generated in the Coded C.I.N. Language." [Law #: 3001330 9/30/2075.] By this point in time the "powers that be" loved making Laws and new "codes', they just needed more and more of the "technology rush." They were never satisfied and were constantly pushing for the next level of human existence.

YEAR: 2090 ...

Pittsburgh has been "Shut Down" by the Council with a Law passed on March 31st 2090, due to a population drop. As there are now fewer than 2 million people left on the planet. Only Rochester and The Dome at Niagara Falls were up and running. With the population being mostly plug-ins at this point in time, as there were less than 5000 Council members and Specialists with their families left. Time was not being kind to these people in charge who were aging very rapidly, and dying off. This was a major problem for these 5000; because they didn't want to die. The answer to that problem was the plug-ins, who were young and could re-produce; that meant a steady flow of life that could be harvested for organs to transplant into the Kings and Queens of the future. So that the Council members and the Specialists could live on; because they believed that they were needed and the plug-ins were not!

At this time Council made a Law which stated that plug-ins would have to become "Organ and Stem Cell Donors to the Council members and the Specialists to keep the World Alive and Well".

LAW # 321000123 was passed on April1st of 2090, which would mean More Law Codes and Dates are sent through the mind of the plug-ins, all by the Code

Makers who also make the Laws, and this is all possible because of Codex Infina-Net the C.I.N. Master Computer Code.

Now the Council members and the Specialists could live well past their 80's, and 90's, the age that all of them were at this time. They could live on by taking organs and stem-cells from young healthy plug-ins. The men and woman who have never been plugged-into the computer; namely the "powers that be," the exact same people who started it all some 40 years ago {in 2050 AD}, were still free thinkers out side of the computer. With the new Law in place these people some in their 90's; the Council members and Specialists, could now live on to maybe 150 years old, or more. That was enough for them, for now anyways; … or so they thought!

In 2097 Dr. Crazsine, now known as Code#0017, discovered NANO LIGHT TRANSFER.[N/L T.] which simply saying was: "merging the electricity within the brain to the Nano-Light in the computer." This would completely merge the mind of man with the computer to create one thinking entity when "plugged-in". With the high-speed electrical energy in the human brain, and the light-speed inside the nano-world of the computer, man could now get to the <u>next level</u> of <u>human evolution</u>. With the final goal that is just around the corner of time, which was; for mankind to "become a God," with the new technology; namely the N/L-T.

A problem arose though; because the early tests of the new N/L-T on plug-ins proved fatal to them. The reason being was the genetically low IQ levels in their brains. This genetic defect would not allow the plug-ins to process all the information coming into their minds at Nano-Speed, and their heads literally "exploded."

Code # 0017 knew that the N/L T. could not be used on the plug-ins, and he also knew that it had to be a Council member or a Specialist who would have to try the N/L-T; because they all had IQ's of 160 or higher. This meant that their brains could probably take the high speed information coming in with nano-light speed! The only problem was that none of them were plug-ins at this point in time, and none of them were in hurry to try it out either. Not even Code # 0017, who invented most of the technology, was willing to plug-in!

YEAR 2100 …

As the 22nd Century arrives in time, so has mankind arrived at the final phase of man becoming one with the fabric of the universe itself. All of this is made possible through the electricity that is permanent and has permeability to the space-time continuum and also to mans brain. In other words man could become a "living 3D person," a holographic being in the space-time. This meant that they could literally "walk to the moon" in real time, and space. This could all be attained by just plugging into the Nano-Light Transfer in Codex InfinaNet; all inside the C.I.N. Master Computer Code!

The Codex InfinaNet Master Computer Code Data-Base [C.I.N.], held the entirety of Human History since the Dawn of Civilization. All historical events were tuned into NANO LIGHT in the Code and with the Neurons in the Brain; both became one Electrical Impulse that would allow the user to enter the Nano-Light Transfer as a Living 3D Being! Who could then walk into the ancient land of Greece in 500 BC or walk into the Roman Empire as Caesar himself, one could be the Queen of Sheba, then again they could travel to Egypt and become the Pharaoh, all done in real space and real time! The digital code of everything when man and the C.I.N. would merge into one; ... or that is what they thought!

Everything that man has done was in the C.I.N. Computer Code because it was all about codes anyways! That's why they were always making new codes with the Laws, and that was why everyone had "codes" instead of names as of 25 years ago! The Council and the Specialists loved the codes and were always searching for the master code in everything!

YEAR 2101 ...

On January 1st at 1 am. in the year 2101 a signal was picked-up on the C.I.N. Computer as it was being contacted by the Edge of the Universe Space-Probe; that was launched into space, in the year 2025. The message was unclear at first, but the signal became stronger as it came in with a report that read:
<>THE UNIVERSE IS A CLOSED SYSTEM> THIS SYSTEM IS ALL A DIGITIZED ELECTRICAL SIMULATION > LIGHT IS A CODE >THERE IS NO GOD! ONLY LIGHT CODES IN THE ELECTRICAL PERMATIV-ITY AND PERMEABILTY OF THE SPACE-TIME CONTINUUM<> END OF SIGNAL<>

By 3 o'clock that same morning the Council and Specialists were discussing this perplexing message that was sent by the Edge of the Universe Space-Probe. In the opening statement of this special session of the powers that be, Code# 0013 began the session by saying:

"If the universe is in a closed system then we are all in a cosmic bubble; correct!" And "YES YES" they all yelled and all agreed. He continued: "Then if Life is a Digital Electrical Simulation of Light, then We can Live Forever in the Nano Light Transfer with the electricity that is in our Brains and the Electricity that makes up the fabric of the Cosmic Bubble!" Once again they all said "YES, YES!"

Then Code# 0013 made his final statement: "There Is No GOD; and if no god, Then We Shall become The Gods and they all screamed "YES, YES, YES, We Can Be As Gods!" Discussion was over; the conclusion was unanimous, which was that the Council members and the Specialists would PLUG-IN, for the first time to the NANO-LIGHT. So they could live forever in the Digital Holographic Universe where they would be Gods and Goddesses!

YEAR 2102 …

By the year 2102 all of the CODES, the Council, and the Specialists were now all Plug-ins to the "Nano-Light" as it was now called. Inside the Nano-Light the new plug-ins were loving every minute of the experience in their ability to become one with the vastness of the Universe' and to travel back in time to live in the past!

While the plug-ins of old continued on in their computer induced activity coded lives; that kept the society buzzing like bees, in the Golden Dome beehive of the only reality that the plug-ins know; … because they are mindless slaves for the system. All the while, the King and the Queen CODES were still making LAWS to control the society, and they now had the technology to live forever; … or so they thought!

New Law December 31st, 2102, which states: All Codes will be known as CODEX HUMANUS when traveling in the Nano-Light … the human race is no longer … we are now CODEX HUMANUS.… Law# 41000961169 12/31/2102

YEAR: 2108 …

On March 22nd of 2108 Code # 0017and Code # 0005 had discovered a way to stay in the Nano-Light longer than the meager 2 hours allowed by the Law; this allowed the highest Codes accsess that other Codes did not have.

Once these higher Codes were in the Light they could stay for as long as three days at a time. The few "chosen ones" were the very tight knit group of pioneers in this World of the Future, and all of them were 100 years old or more by now. There were only 20 of them in control of the earth at this juncture in time. At this point they thought themselves to be Gods and made a Law that stated: "Only the Highest codes are Chosen Ones and can enter the Nano-Light" … LAW CODE CIN # 1 …

This meant that any Code above the number 20 was now just a regular "plug-in." This new law gave to the 20 members out of the 1000 members the only access to the Nano-Light Transfer. In total were 980 former Council members and Specialists who were now X-Codes; just another number in the mindless working lives of the plug-ins.

With the "Chosen Ones" totaling only 20, out of the 2 million people left on the earth. With this small group being the only ones able to enter the Light for a Three Day journey into the past. Becoming a 3D living holographic Person in real Space and Time! Now the chosen ones were traveling as often as they could; because they just loved the power trip that they were on!

In their travels they always returned to Ancient Greece, Rome, Egypt, and their favorite destination which is Atlantis. With all the 1000's of years in man-kind's recorded history that is stored in the C.I.N. Computer, they chose to be in the land of the Ancients who lived as far back as 7000 years ago. One of the rea-sons for choosing these past locations was that they were intrigued by the gods in antiquity, and the fact that they were being worshiped by their own ancestors. Every trip back in time was a game to these "chosen ones" because they could "pop-in" and "pop-out" of reality right in front of the ancients; who by seeing this would fall on their faces in reverence to the gods. Who were of course them-selves! With each new trip back in time they were discovering that they were and are the gods of the past. The "chosen ones" from the "future" are the gods of the past.

A problem arose with the fact that they could only stay in the past for three days at a time, and they desired to stay longer; but for now this would suffice; … or so they thought!

The Chosen Ones had figured out that they, the 20 themselves, were all of the gods from history, Zeus, Apollo, RA, Diana, Aphrodite and even the God of Numbers from Atlantis named Xedoc. All the real gods of the past according to the C.I.N Computer Code were actually the Men and Women of the Future traveling backwards in time!

All this was made possible by the Nano-Light and the C.I.N. Computer Code working inside the mind of man, as they traveled into the Cosmic Bubble {the Universe} in an Electrical Simulation. A Digital Reality with the Past, the Present and the Future all occurring at the same time, all inside the sub-atomic world of man with machine! The Men and Women from the future were the gods of the past, and they loved every minute of the experience. Man had to answer to no god because they were God.

For the "chosen ones" to gain the understanding from their own "technology with science"; that there is "NO Creator GOD," and also realizing from their time travel into the past; … that they were THE GODS. They now knew from all of their own genius that eternal heaven was in their reach; yes: mankind was now what he and she reasoned to be so long ago. Man was God, ... or so he thought! Then mankind made his final Law by Choice.

NEW and LAST LAW: "WE ... THE CHOSEN ONES ... ARE THE GODS OF THE PAST ... THE PRESENT ... and FOREVER ... ALL INFORMATION IN THE CODEX INFINANET THAT REFERENCES ANY CREATOR GOD ... THE BIBLE ... AND ALL HOLY BOOKS ... WILL BE DELETED ... WE ARE THE GODS OF LIGHT" ... Date only: June 21st, 2108 ...

YEAR: 2109 ...

The City of Rochester was Shut-Down on September 22nd due to the shrinking population and the fact that one of the Nano Light's at the Rochester Institute for Mind Research melted-down; the cause is still unknown! All plug-ins and the Chosen Ones moved to The Niagara Dome, as now this was the last City on Earth.

Population 144,000 and 20!

YEAR: 2110 ...

January 1st 2110 the remnant of mankind and his civilization is now all living under the Golden Magnetic Dome that is covering all of the City of Niagara Falls. The main C.I.N Nano-Light Transfer Computer was brought from Rochester and the Gods {chosen ones} were using it more and more, and more. They all took names from the gods that they believed they were in the past. Code # 0013 became Zeus, Code# 0010 became Apollo, and so it was, all of them took the names of Ancient gods, ... because that's who they thought they really were!

Back and forth they traveled in time to teach the people of the Past their wisdom of mathematics, building techniques and the Universe; they taught them with all of the knowledge from the C.I.N computer of the Future. These men and women from the future {Gods} could teach the Ancients just like the history in the C.I.N. Data-Base has said that they had! They traveled so often that they were spending less time monitoring the "plug-ins" but that was O.K.; because the C.I.N did all the programming with the Codes anyway. So the Gods were happy and the 144,000 plug-ins were just as "mindlessly" content like: busy bees making honey, all under the Golden Dome of man.

With the C.I.N Computer in control this allowed the Gods to travel all the time to the past, and stay even longer than the Three Day Maximum. They would stay for weeks at a time, even though this usage would over load the C.I.N. computer. Code #0017, who was now Xedoc from Atlantis, the inventor of all the technology that brought man to his rightful place as Gods, he at one point told the others: "not to travel for extended periods of time; because of the over-load factors involved." They did not want to listen to him because; they were Gods and they did not listen to other Gods, it was that simple; … or so they thought.

This is where the fighting started, something that had not been on the earth for over 80 years. This 1st war in the 22nd century was being fought in the Digital Electricity of Nano-Light; as the Mind of Man and The Universe became one inside the C.I.N. Computer. Date Only: December 7th … 2110 …

YEAR: 2111 …

MONTH: JANUARY 1st, 2111 … 8:00 AM …

As the New Year arrived the Gods were traveling all the time now, not to teach anymore; No they went back in time to argue and fight. All of them had a disregard for the warnings that the system could over-load, they just followed eachother from Greece to Rome, and from Egypt to Atlantis. Back and forth all the time, and fighting constantly about who would be the NUMBER ONE GOD IN THE COSMIC BUBBLE OF SPACE TIME, THE GOD OF IT ALL. They argued and fought all the time, 24 hours a day, all inside of the Nano-Light in which they were living in full time now. They even left the plug-ins to themselves, and they left the Past also; all so they could confront each other in the Darkest Part Of The Light to see who would be the GOD of GODS.

MONTH: JUNE 6th, 2111 … 9:00 AM …

From the first of the year until now, 6 months later, there has been non-stop fighting going on inside the Nano-Light with all of the gods. By them staying in the Nano Light for this long; the C.I.N. computer is in near melt-down mode. With them being so deep inside the Computer itself, as the mind, machine, and light become one, nobody seems to be watching, as the system is nearing the "critical Red-Zone." As they are all too busy fighting amongst eachother about who would be the true god.

All this fighting went on inside the electrical simulation of the C.I.N. Computer, where the holographic Gods battled for supremacy in the Digital Universe that is all made of Light Codes. Each one believed this to be the true reality: that everything was electrical impulses of light, and it was all in codes.

There had to be more though, and so they fought even more, and the C.I.N. was heating up even more; … to the Critical Red Zone! As the Nano-Light was heating up towards Critical Red many of the gods fled to the outer darkness of the N/L-T C.I N.!

They could not go back to their own reality at this point in time; because the exit port-hole had been "shut-down." Now they were stuck in the "wild" areas of "space-time" where "demons and dragons" live!

MONTH: AUGUST 9th, 2111 … 10:09 AM …

Only Zeus, Apollo, Diana, and Xedoc were left in the ring for this round of the fight, all in the deepest level of the C.I.N. Computer, and as this war of the Gods was heating up, so was the C.I.N. Computer. As the battle of the Titans roared, and the other Gods were fleeing to the "outer darkness;" out of nowhere an unidentified CODE breaks into the C.I.N. Master Computer with this message:

"ATLANTIS: LOST CIVILIZATION?" That was it; and the message ended just as abruptly as it came! What did the message mean, who was this "Unidentified Code", was there some sort of "new energy" in the space-time continuum that they did not know about? These questions brought the "gods" back into a cooperative mood, as the fighting stopped. Then they started debating the who, what, and why of the bizarre message. The first thing they did was to travel back in time to Atlantis where they could look for any clues that would de-code the message from the unknown.

MONTH: SEPTEMBER 10th, 9:00 … AM. 2111 …

After spending a month looking for clues the gods return from Atlantis with just as much information as they left with; which was Nothing! The debate about the mysterious intruder and the message continued non-stop in the Nano-Light Transfer. Every minute of every day, and still no answers about what the message meant. They debated and searched the C.I.N Data-Base over, and over again; which gave no new insight into their perplexing problem at hand! As the investigation came to a standstill a new message scrolled into their minds.

Just as the first mysterious Code "Popped-In" to visit, so did the second one in the same way. The message this time was in Code and said: "E/A-e/a-E/A." That was it, nothing more.

To Zeus, Apollo, Diana and Xedoc this made less sense than the first message, but at least it was a "letter code" like the DNA molecule, so they could most likely figure out the meaning of the Code.

Apollo thought that it could be an "electrical flux" generating random Codes in the Cosmic Bubble. Diana believed it was an "anomaly" in the space-time continuum. Zeus said it had to be: "a random number generated deep within the C.I.N. Computer". Then Xedoc conjectured that it must be a "being from hyperspace," outside of the known Cosmic Electrical Light Bubble that they were living in! Four Gods, with four different answers, this caused the fighting to start up all over again, but this time it was much worst; as Diana and Apollo were "Un-Plugged" by Zeus! [they were the only two in history to be "un-plugged"]

That left only two gods, and the unidentifiable code all inside the Nano-Light Transfer; ... and then there were three!

MONTH: OCTOBER, 1st, 2111 ... 12:00 PM ...

As Xedoc and Zeus continued their argueing the Domed City of Niagara is devastated by a 9.0 earthquake which destroyed most of the city, and caused a build up of "electro-magnetism" in the Nano-Light, and the Main C.I.N Computer was about to Melt-Down!

Zeus and Xedoc ignored all of this and fought even more as their anger grew "Red Hot" towards one another. Even though they still had no answer on Who or What the New Code or Coder were up to! To these two nothing mattered except being the only God in the known Cosmic Bubble of Light, to be the solo player in History, as the Almighty GOD. Who would it be, Xedoc or Zeus? They both knew that whoever De-Coded the message first would win the war of Supremacy, and all of Eternity would be theirs!

OCTOBER 31st, 2111 ... 11:59:59 PM ... Tic ...

As the Clock Struck Mid-Night: just then in an instant the Unknown Code Flashed its final message: "CODE # 6 6 6 ... YOU ... LOSE!!! SHORT CIRCUIT ... THERE IS NO LIGHT ... ONLY DARKNESS ... I MAKE THE LAW ... IT'S OVER>>>>>>>>>> >>>>>>>>>>>>>>>>>>>>>>>>>>>
Then An Eternal Silence...

THINK ABOUT THIS:

The Clock hit 00:00 at Mid-Night on October 31st 2111 AD., had Time run out, or did a new Clock start? Did Mankind move so deep into His own Mind, that He could not escape, or did the C.I.N. Computer become such a part of Man that it would not let Him go? Until the Final instant; when all was gone for good!

One small speck of Light in Time that was consumed by the "empty Darkness", not just a history lost in time, no, no, no, this history never was in time! When man had traveled so deep inside the C.I.N. Computer that his whole reality was an illusion inside the machine, had he wandered too deep? When Man "plugged-in" he gave up his Body to become a Digital 3 D person, little did he know that not only did he lose his body, but the Soul that was there too! Even with all the knowledge that they had in the Future; they could not Out-Smart the C.I.N Master, who had finally won in the end. As Man thought in his heart to be "AS GODS" inside the Computer, Mans destiny by choice led them to the "Outer-Darkness!"

For all the choices Man could have made; He chose to "Be as GODS' and He made the Technology to do it! Man did not remember that the Master of the C.I.N. CODE {Satan} had said this before; which was that He would sit on "GODS Thrown!" The people of the Future would have recognized Him, but they Deleted the Bible from their Hearts, and Minds, and even from their own Codes!

The Code was there all the time in the <u>Book of Revelation</u>; <u>chapter 13</u>: verse <u>18</u>, which reads: "<u>Here is Wisdom, let him that has understanding count the number of the Beast: for it is the number of a Man: and His number is Six hundred threescore and Six</u>:" [666, The man made beast ... the C.I.N computer ... gave cover for the real S I N master to hide in, ... that would be Satan]

Man did not have the Wisdom to Count the Code, because he threw out the Bible, and then the C.I.N. Computer Code Number of the Beast devoured everything on "The Planet of the Plug-Ins!"

Remember the Coded Message given on Sebt. 10th of 2111, at 9:00 AM which was; "EA/-ea-/Ea;" Lets decipher the Code: E = the 5th letter of the alphabet, A = the 1st letter ... The Code is: 5 + 1 = 6. EA/-e/a-E/A = 6 6 6 ... THIS FUTURE CLOCK STOPS ... TIC ... TIC ... TIC ... RIGHT NOW! ... THE END!

Conclusion

Are the <u>Past</u>, the <u>Present</u>, and the <u>Future</u> all "<u>running</u> "at the <u>same time</u>? It doesn't seem that way when we are in the "Now", but the Past will always be a part of the Present, and who ever lives until tomorrow is part of the Future. Can you see that all three Clocks, Past, Present, and Future, are all "running" at the same Time! All rolled up in the harmony of "what was, what is, and what will be." The pendulum of Time swinging back and forth keeping the Cosmic Rhythm of what we've done, what we are doing, and what we might end up doing. <u>All three clocks are forever linked together.</u>

Will we as the human race become a Lost Civilization like Atlantis, a modern society from the past that is only an archeological "Dig" in the Future, or do we become the Planet of the Plug-Ins? Will we throw out the Bible and become; a Planet Hell Bent, and Hell Bound, when man plays GOD!

Will the human race learn to live in peace? To answer that, ask yourself this first: "Is the Earth a War Machine"? The answer from history is "YES", Earth is a War Machine; but will the war of the future be fought in our minds and hearts, instead of on the battle field, ... or will it even matter in the Future if a person has a Mind or a Heart? Only time will tell; but Time is "Running Out!"

The most brilliant minds of our day say that the Universe had a beginning; they call this the Big-Bang Theory, now if the Universe had a beginning that means it will have an Ending; this is called by scientists "The Ultimate Heat-Death." This is when all matter and energy have a uniform temperature; which simply saying is "all three Clocks of Time will Stop, and this will be The End of Time As we Know it!

When Time will stand no more then: Whose Time Was It Anyway? When the Universe dies of the Heat-Death will all of Time and History be "Erased"; will the "<u>Human Experience</u>" all have been for nothing?

The truth is today we know that the Universe is going to die, just like you and I, as we will all take that journey some day. What will happen to Us and the Universe when everything dies? We know from science that everything in the Universe, including us, works with some form of "electricity" the Spark of Life and Energy!

According to the theory of Relativity "energy and matter" can not be <u>created</u> or <u>destroyed</u> they can only <u>change</u> their forms to other <u>matter</u>, and or <u>energy</u>; including maybe even light!

This means that all energy in the universe including us is a form of "energy" and we can not be destroyed we shall only "change" forms. This means that yours, and mine, the Electrical spark of Life is going to last forever and so is the Universe. They must first die; and then they will change forms to an Eternal State! In simple terms you and I will last after death, and the laws of science prove it.

If we are going to last Forever then the question is; where does the Spark of Life, our Energy go to when we die?

THINK ABOUT THIS:

"I saw a new heaven and a new earth: for the first earth and the first heaven were passed away:" This statement is about the universe being renewed after the Heat-Death that Scientists know will happen!

"The Truth I say to you: except a seed of wheat fall into the ground and die; it is alone; but if it dies; it brings forth much fruit" This statement says that all living things, even down to the tiniest seed bring forth Energy Fruit [Life], first it has to die and then life is renewed, in another form. First the seed goes in the ground dormant, and then in time it grows into a giant life giving wheat stalk; far different than the small dead seed.

Once again, this is in agreement with modern science that says; "Life s Energy will be Reborn in another Form somewhere else, after Death." Even Science states that the "Energy:" read that THE SOUL OR SPIRIT, will LAST FOREVER, WOW!

Both of the underlined statements above come from the Bible, the first one is from the Book of Revelation [21:1], and the other is found in the Gospel of John [12:24], and both statements are scientifically provable, in theory only, because no one has visited the other side and come back from the dead to explain everything about the after-life to us; or has someone done just that.

History tells us that Jesus Christ did die on the cross and rose again, on the third day, to everlasting life in a new resurrected body! A change in the physical matter that made up His body and the Electrical Spark that is His Spirit, Jesus' new resurrected body and spirit living on in eternity!

Modern science and the Bible both agree on this: modern science states that the electrical spark in everything will last forever; the Bible has said all along that "Life is Eternal." ... I would like to ask: "How did the men who wrote the Bible know all this "scientific" inside Info.; as we have just discovered all of this today with Modern Mathematics which is this FACT: Energy is Eternal!"

My case in point to where we go after we die is "Get use to the idea that You and I are Eternal; which modern science and the Bible agree on is that ......

"WE are going to be around FOREVER." Get use to that idea and make your choice in this life on where you end up going for eternity.

If GOD Himself came down to the Earth right now in 2007, what would He say to us?

Would GOD say: "SO YOU FIGURED OUT THAT YOUR ENERGY WILL LAST FOREVER: I TOLD YOU THAT IN MY WORD AT THE BEGINNING OF TIME. THE PAST: THE PRESENT: AND THE FUTURE: ARE ALL IN MY HANDS, I AM THE FIRST TIC ON THE CLOCK AND THE LAST; I ALONE AM THE HANDS OF TIME; NOW; WHOSE TIME IS IT.... ANYWAY"

DID I, EVEN I, GET MY POINT <u>ACROSS</u> OR WILL I HAVE TO <u>HANG</u> HERE AND WATCH UNTIL THE <u>TRUTH</u> IS NAILED INTO YOUR <u>HEARTS</u>; THEN THE CROWN OF PEACE CLEARS YOUR MIND, AND IN MY LAST BREATH; YOU MY SONS AND DAUGTHERS WHOM I <u>LOVE</u>; YOU SHALL HAVE <u>LIFE</u>: <u>ETERNAL</u>!" "<u>I AM THE LORD ... JESUS CHRIST</u>"

The Clocks of Time are they a cosmic accident or by a Divine Creation; are the Clocks of Time just random tics in the Universe, or did Gods Hands start the hands of Time? That question can only be answered by you! Do you Believe or Not Believe in GOD; this is the ultimate question; well not completely. The other part of the question is; which God? That is were the answer is; it is in the question: "WHOSE TIME IS IT ANYWAY; GODS or man? Jesus Christ or false gods; you decide, for that is your sovereign choice!

I pray that you have had an interesting journey in Time with "One mans view of our Human Experience", and may all of your "Experiences in your travels of life be peaceful, and look-up for GOD, as He Shines down His LOVE upon thee!"

Oh, no, so Sorry, I have to run; my computer just Crashed! Oh well, that's modern technology for ya'! Hey I think I can Claim that on my Car Insurance, it was a "Crash" and that's an "Accident;" RIGHT? O.K. I was a little carried away; it was just a thought! ... Think about it, and you'll have the time; as now I have run out of paper to type on, and that's lucky for you. So I will conclude now by saying: "Let Jesus be your guide in life, the journey is a lot easier down here.

Why not let The LORD be the beating force in your Heart! Think about it: Peace My Friend!"

THE END!

P.S. ... "I am the light of the world: those who follow me shall not walk in the darkness, but shall have the light of life" ... words from Jesus Christ ... and always remember: there are no clocks in heaven ... Whose Time Is It ? Anyway ...!
Jesus Christ Wants You:
sign-up;...............

978-0-595-43367-4
0-595-43367-7